RAND ARROYO CENTER

T0302569

China's Expanding African Relations

Implications for U.S. National Security

Lloyd Thrall

Prepared for the United States Army

For more information on this publication, visit www.rand.org/t/rr905

Library of Congress Cataloging-in-Publication Data is available for this publication.

ISBN 978-0-8330-8850-5

Published by the RAND Corporation, Santa Monica, Calif.

Preface

The U.S. Army asked the RAND Arroyo Center to examine several aspects of the evolving security landscape and potential effects on U.S. national security involvement in Africa through a project titled "Army Force and Resource Requirements to Support AFRICOM." This effort resulted in this report, as well as a companion report by Stephen Watts titled *Identifying and Mitigating Risks in Security Sector Assistance for Africa's Fragile States* (RR-808-A).

This report examines how China's rapidly growing engagement with African states affects the U.S. Army's role on the continent, and it offers policy recommendations for U.S. and Army leaders. While China's engagement with Africa is frequently caricatured as monolithic and geostrategic, this report acknowledges the diversity of Chinese actors interacting with counterparts across 54 African states. It also acknowledges the active role that Africans play in shaping the relationship, as well as the lack of centralized control from Beijing over many Chinese actors. This report should be of interest to U.S. Army and Department of Defense personnel involved in planning related to Africa or China's overseas policies, as well as to broader communities of interest concerned with these subjects.

This research was sponsored by the Deputy Chief of Staff, G-8, U.S. Army, and conducted within the RAND Arroyo Center's Strategy and Resources Program. RAND Arroyo Center, part of the RAND Corporation, is a federally funded research and development center sponsored by the United States Army.

The Project Unique Identification Code (PUIC) for the project that produced this document is HQD126409.

Research questions and comments should be directed to project leader Karl Mueller at mueller@rand.org or the Director of the Strategy and Resources Program, Terrence Kelly, at tkelly@rand.org. For more information about the RAND Arroyo Center, contact the Director of Operations (telephone 310-393-0411, extension 6419; fax 310-451-6952; email Marcy_Agmon@rand.org), or visit Arroyo's web site at http://www.rand.org/ard.

Contents

Figures and Table

Figures

Table

Summary

The explosive growth in Sino-African relations over the past decade has heightened U.S. trepidation over China's role in Africa. Across economic, political, and security domains, the growth of China's presence has been swift and staggering. For example, Sino-African trade increased almost twentyfold since 2000, supplanting the United States as the continent's largest trading partner. Among the permanent United Nations (U.N.) Security Council members, China's People's Liberation Army (PLA) is the largest contributor to U.N. peacekeeping in Africa, deploying 20 times the number of peacekeepers it sent to Africa in 2000. In addition, approximately 1 million Chinese live in Africa, up from only a few thousand ten years ago. In sum, China's emergence is probably the most significant geopolitical and economic event on the continent since the conclusion of the Cold War. Such sudden growth, occurring alongside Sino-American tensions in Asia, has fed both simplistic caricatures of China's role in Africa and fears of renewed geopolitical competition in Africa. A closer look reveals a more balanced picture that is diverse, multifaceted, and evolving.

China's engagement with Africa is not new, though it is has grown and evolved substantially. Chinese engagement during the Maoist period was strongly ideological and geopolitical. Reflecting the economic and political realities of post-Mao China, China's economic interests have gradually ascended as the primary drivers of its behavior in Africa. While the rhetorical themes of solidarity and anti-imperialism continue in Chinese rhetoric, current Chinese engagement with African states is nonideological; Beijing engages readily with socialist, free-market, democratic, authoritarian, and theocratic regimes alike. While economic interests tend to dominate, a range of stakeholders and interests drive contemporary Chinese behavior in Africa, often in tension with each other.

Economic Interests and Behavior

China's government and commercial actors have three primary economic interests in Africa: a source for natural resource imports, a growing and relatively underutilized market for exports and investment, and an opportunity for Chinese firms to increase employment and gain global experience. China's investment in Africa occurs in the broader context of Beijing's "Go Global" (走出去) commercial strategy, intended to increase outgoing Chinese investment and commercial presence. Contrary to the model of Chinese firm operations being driven by Beijing's geopolitical strategy, the vast majority of Chinese economic interactions in Africa are profit-driven, and Beijing has struggled to maintain oversight of its firms' overseas activities.

Natural resource imports are China's largest economic interest in Africa, and these resources constitute about 90 percent of African exports to industrialized states. China, however, has imported far less African oil than the United States or European Union over the last ten years, with far more balanced trade than either. Cumulative Chinese oil-firm investment in Africa remains less than 10 percent of such Western firm investment, typically on the fringes of Africa's oil landscape. China's hydrocarbon investment in Africa does not threaten U.S. or global energy security but instead brings new oil to market while functionally reducing Chinese demand. Similarly, the potential for Sino-American conflict over African resources is extremely remote.

Sino-African economic relations vary greatly, based primarily on whether the African state has natural resources and a market for Chinese goods. While no state is in a position to monopolize Africa's trade, China has become the largest trade partner for Africa as a whole (though second to an aggregated European Union). China remains the largest exporter of small arms and light weapons to African states.

Sino-African economic relations are generally of greater importance to African states than to China; Sino-African trade accounts for 15 percent of African states' total, but just 5 percent of China's total trade. With respect to finance, despite persistent problems with data availability and reliability, China has emerged as a major source of financial capital. The vast majority of Chinese investment and loan activity is profit-driven and succeeds on its own commercial merits, rather than as a state-directed foreign policy tool. South Africa remains China's most important economic relationship in Africa, constituting more than one-third of Sino-African trade and the leading destination on the continent for Chinese foreign direct investment.

Political Interests and Behavior

Beijing has four principal political interests in Africa: bolstering China's international image and influence, isolating Taiwan, countering problematic international norms, and supporting the stability of economic partners.

Beijing has gone to great lengths to emphasize a "peaceful development" of Chinese power.[1] Outreach efforts in Africa can increase the credibility of this image, as well as reap tangible diplomatic benefits through African support. While diplomatic competition with Taiwan is relatively dormant, Beijing has a continuing interest in isolating Taipei, now recognized by only three African states. With regard to international norms, African support can assist Beijing in countering precedents that China views as potentially dangerous domestically. From both a legal and diplomatic perspective, Beijing likely perceives an interest in preventing international activism on issues of democratic governance and human rights intervention in Africa that could apply equally to domestic Chinese political order. China's stance of not interfering in domestic governance and human rights issues is often appre-

[1] Information Office of the State Council, *China's Peaceful Development Road*, White Paper, Beijing: Ministry of National Defense of the People's Republic of China, December 22, 2005.

ciated and reciprocated by African governments, even among those with democratic traditions and solid human rights practices. Finally, Beijing has a growing interest in African stability commensurate with its growing economic and political investment there and its desire to be seen as a responsible global power.

Over the past ten years, Beijing has been busier than Washington in political engagement with African states, including three times as many head-of-state visits as the George W. Bush and Barack Obama administrations during that span. While China's relations with African states are for the most part bilateral, the triennial Forum on China-Africa Cooperation is the centerpiece of Chinese multilateral engagement with African states, bringing together heads of state and ministry-level leaders. Alongside senior-level engagement has been a significant increase in mid-level outreach and soft-power initiatives. This has included several notable building projects (including the African Union Headquarters) and a significant expansion of Chinese state media in Africa. Contrary to much Western press reporting, African heads of state tend to make sunnier statements toward China than toward the United States, and opinion polls show generally positive views of China on the continent.

Security Interests and Behavior

China's emerging security interests in Africa are driven by Beijing's larger interests in safeguarding economic development and increasing political influence. Beijing's conception of its security interests has continued to grow; this is best evidenced by the 2004 introduction of "New Historic Missions" (新的历史使命) for the PLA that highlight China's expanding global interests and role in "safeguarding world peace and promoting common development."[2] As a regional power with expanding global interests, China is in the process of defining its security interests in some of the world's most unstable areas. Chinese firms have

---

[2] Cortez A. Cooper, *The PLA Navy's "New Historic Missions"—Expanding Capabilities for a Re-emergent Maritime Power*, Santa Monica, Calif.: RAND Corporation, CT-332, 2009.

active investments and contracts of more than $1 billion in 12 of the world's top 20 failed or failing states. Beijing's foremost emerging security interest is protecting the growing number of citizens and assets from internal instability, popular backlash, terrorism, and kidnapping. Terrorist groups have conducted or pledged attacks against Chinese citizens with increasing frequency, particularly in North Africa. Beijing's remaining security interests in Africa are to buoy its reputation as a global leader and increase the operational experience of a PLA that has little. To date, however, Beijing has taken remarkably little interest in directly exporting security and has continued its public commitment not to develop overseas bases. This likely stems from three factors: the PLA's current limitations in power projection, fear of international perceptions of a "China threat,"[3] and Beijing's diplomatic commitment to not intervene in the affairs of other states.

The largest area of Chinese military engagement with Africa has been PLA participation in U.N. peacekeeping operations. After a long period of eschewing and criticizing such participation as foreign interference, the PLA currently participates in seven of the eight U.N. missions in Africa. The PLA has also expanded bilateral military diplomacy, though it remains far behind Western militaries. Africa has been the location for some of the PLA's most prominent global operations: the ongoing 2008 Gulf of Aden counterpiracy deployment, the 2011 noncombatant evacuation from Libya, and the 2013 deployments of PLA infantry to U.N. missions to Mali and South Sudan. These events represent notable firsts for the PLA, suggesting future growth in PLA roles and capabilities, albeit unlikely to be as robust as Western military involvement in Africa.

Future Developments and Sino-American Interest Correlation

China's engagement with Africa has changed dramatically over the past ten years and will likely continue to do so. Most importantly, Chi-

---

[3] Xia Ming, "'China Threat' or a 'Peaceful Rise of China'?" *New York Times*, undated.

na's growing African interests will probably complicate Beijing's ability to remain agnostic about the internal affairs of African states. China's strict nonintervention approach reflects political realities now more than five decades old. Growing and diversifying interests, as well as the proliferation of Chinese actors in Africa and Beijing's imperfect control of them, will probably precipitate a modest growth in Chinese involvement in African states' regional relationships and domestic affairs.

Specifically, Beijing is likely to face sensitive state failures, overtly anti-Chinese popular movements, terrorism, and kidnappings with increased frequency. Regarding economic relations, the explosive growth of the previous decade should slow as Chinese growth slows and the surge of capital released by the "Go Global" policy subsides. Beijing may have to navigate issues of debt sustainability with African states if economic ties do not balance. Regarding security, significant mismanagement of security crises in Africa could put Beijing's domestic legitimacy and its principles of foreign noninterference in tension. While not likely in the next decade, Beijing could create a minimally invasive capability for reacting to crises, evacuating citizens, and securing assets in Africa. However, concerns over China developing a network of forward naval bases seem misplaced.

Unlike the zero-sum geopolitical competition that defined the Cold War in Africa, contemporary Sino-American interests in Africa are far less divergent and less dangerous. The United States and China share a fundamental interest in the stability of African states and functioning markets as a prerequisite for the economic benefits, deepening relationships, and global leadership image that each hopes to portray. Neither state is promoting political ideologies or mercantilist economic aims that would naturally lead toward conflict in the region. Washington and Beijing disagree about the most effective way of achieving stability and growth, reflecting their domestic political structures and development histories. Neither state, however, is inflexible in the application of its development philosophy. U.S. and Chinese interests diverge most seriously over the role of foreign powers in supporting good governance and human rights norms in Africa, particularly regarding pariah states. While Beijing has blunted international pressure on such states as Sudan and Zimbabwe, it has also used its closer relationship with such states to curb their behavior when it too seriously threatened stability or Beijing's international reputation.

Most importantly, African states will continue to balance their relations and remain selective consumers of foreign states' overtures. Neither state will play the lead in any transformation of African economies or political order; that role will continue to be filled by African leaders.

Conclusions and Policy Recommendations

China's unfavorable activities in Africa should be viewed in context. U.S. and Chinese critics both tend to compare an idealized version of their own involvement in Africa with a selective criticism of the other's activities. Struggles against authoritarianism and illiberalism in Africa, with decidedly mixed results, long predate China's new role on the continent. Further, while not to the degree of China, the United States and Europe continue to pursue relations with authoritarian regimes and have struggled to regulate commercial behavior. Given the degree to which Beijing struggles to control its subordinate economic actors, the United States should resist the desire to divine Beijing's strategic intent from each action. The growth of Chinese influence is not limitless and will not displace a fundamental role for the United States and Europe, particularly in political and security affairs.

Policymakers should avoid elevating low-level competition to bilateral strategic tension and should seek to insulate Sino-American relations in Africa from broader currents in the bilateral relationship. A China that invests in pariah states and resists international human rights norms in Africa is not ideal, but it does not pose an exceptional threat to American interests. Sino-African relations have strong economic foundations that are unlikely to erode, and China's approach to African governance reflects deep roots in China's domestic political structure and history. Zero-sum approaches and adversarial rhetoric are unlikely to be useful. Such an approach also suggests to African states that U.S. relations are skewed toward balance of power politics rather than genuine partnership, while increasing the space for African states to play the United

States and China against one another. To support U.S. leadership in Africa and strengthen international norms, the United States should focus on reinvigorating its African relationships rather than fostering competition with China.

Finally, the United States Africa Command (AFRICOM) should seek opportunities for greater engagement with the PLA in Africa. Despite deep levels of strategic distrust (particularly from Beijing), the emerging security threats that the PLA will face in Africa are familiar to the U.S. Army, increasing the potential for engagement. Such a move would undercut containment rhetoric, demonstrate the value of reduced tensions, and lessen anxiety in African capitals over great-power rivalry. The U.S. Army is best positioned among the services to lead such an engagement initiative. While the relationships of both countries' navies and air forces are focused on the more conflicted dimensions of anti-access/area denial and AirSea Battle in the Pacific, the two ground forces have comparatively fewer areas of direct opposition. The PLA has historically been the preeminent service within the Chinese military, but the focus on the Pacific theater has increased the focus on China's navy, air force, and missile assets (organized outside the PLA, under the Second Artillery Corps). The U.S. Army is looking for a larger role in rebalancing to the Pacific; taking a lead in military diplomacy through army-to-army relations, starting in Africa, may prove valuable to the wider relationship.

Acknowledgments

We wish to express our gratitude to several experts who provided invaluable guidance and assistance during this study. Dr. Deborah Brautigam provided several key insights in the early stages of this research. Dr. Derek Scissors helped our research team navigate the complexities of China's financial relations with African states and actors. J. R. Mailey at the National Defense University provided broad expertise on China's role in Africa, as well as valuable depth on the role of private Chinese actors in commercial relations. Dr. Robert Sutter gave an exceptional review of the text, improving it markedly, as did RAND's Stephanie Pezard and Michael Shurkin. This effort also benefited greatly from parallel analysis being conducted by Larry Hanauer and Lyle Morris in RAND's National Defense Research Institute. In particular, Mr. Morris's willingness to review multiple iterations and discuss the complexities and ambiguities of this subject enhanced our research significantly.

Abbreviations

AFRICOM	United States Africa Command
ANC	African National Congress
BRIC	Brazil, Russia, India, and China
CCP	Chinese Communist Party
DRC	Democratic Republic of the Congo
ECOWAS	Economic Community of West African States
FDI	foreign direct investment
FOCAC	Forum on China-Africa Cooperation
GDP	gross domestic product
IMF	International Monetary Fund
IOSC	Information Office of the State Council
MINUSMA	U.N. Mission in Mali
mbpd	million barrels per day
NEO	noncombatant evacuation operation
NOC	national oil company
OECD	Organisation for Economic Co-operation and Development
PAC	Pan-Africanist Congress
PLA	People's Liberation Army
PLAN	People's Liberation Army Navy
PRC	People's Republic of China

PUIC	Project Unique Identification
SEZ	special economic zone
SOE	state-owned enterprise
U.N.	United Nations
UNMISS	U.N. Mission to South Sudan
WTO	World Trade Organization

CHAPTER ONE

Introduction and Historical Antecedents

Introduction

The explosive growth in Sino-African relations over the past decade has heightened trepidation about China's role in Africa. Of the more than 5 million Chinese citizens living overseas, approximately 1 million live in Africa, up from only a few thousand ten years ago.[1] China's People's Liberation Army (PLA) has 20 times the number of peacekeepers in Africa now than it did in 2000, and it is the largest contributor among the permanent United Nations (U.N.) Security Council members.[2] Sino-African trade increased almost twentyfold over the same period, from $10 billion in 2000 to more than $180 billion in 2012, with China supplanting the United States in 2010 as Africa's largest trading partner.[3] Investment and capital flows have seen a simi-

[1] China's Vice Foreign Minister recently estimated the number of small-scale Chinese entrepreneurs in Africa at "between one and two million" (see David Shinn, "China and Africa in the Xi Jinping Era," *The Diplomat*, March 25, 2013, p. 25). See also *The Economist*, "Africa and China: More Than Minerals," March 23, 2013. For more information on total Chinese citizens living abroad and security threats, see Andrew Erickson, "China's Political and Security Challenges in the Middle East," testimony to the U.S.-China Economic and Security Review Commission hearing on China and the Middle East, June 6, 2013.

[2] Ton Deitz, Kjell Havnevik, Mayke Kaag, and Terje Oestigaard, eds., *African Engagements: Africa Negotiating an Emerging Multipolar World*, Boston, Mass.: Brill Publishers, 2011, p. 214.

[3] David E. Brown, *Hidden Dragon, Crouching Lion: How China's Advance in Africa Is Underestimated and Africa's Potential Underappreciated*, Carlisle, Pa.: Strategic Studies Institute, U.S. Army War College, 2012, p. 10. For trade data, see International Monetary Fund (IMF), "Direction of Trade Statistics (DOTS)," web tool, undated; United Nations, "Com-

lar expansion, quickly elevating China to a position among Africa's leading financiers.[4]

Such rapid growth, occurring alongside Sino-American tensions in Asia, has fed both simplistic characterizations of China's role in Africa and fears of renewed geopolitical competition on the continent. A closer look reveals a more complex and less foreboding picture. Sino-African relations are diverse, multifaceted, and evolving. They involve a varied set of Chinese and African actors across 54 African states, so caution should be taken when attempting to generalize across these relationships. U.S., Chinese, and African sources have often reduced Sino-African relations to enduring caricatures and sweeping generalizations that obscure more than they explain. Chinese sources often view Americans as demonizing Chinese behavior in Africa to support containment and *realpolitik*;[5] U.S. sources tend to view China as exploiting African resources with little care for balanced trade or African stability.[6] Both images are incomplete and inaccurate. Africa's complexity and diversity, rapid change in China's overseas economic interactions, and a growing sense of Sino-American competition have contributed to such distortions. Several exogenous narratives have also contributed—"peak oil," colonial and neocolonial exploitation, mercantilism, and containment, to name a few. In truth, China's emergence in Africa is perhaps the most significant geopolitical and economic event on the

---

trade Database," web tool, undated(a); and United Nations Conference on Trade and Development (UNCTAD), "Statistics," web tool, undated(a).

4 Lauren Gamache, Alexander Hammer, and Lin Jones, "China's Trade and Investment Relationship with Africa," U.S. International Trade Commission, Executive Briefings on Trade, April 2013; U.S. Government Accountability Office, *Sub-Saharan Africa: Trends in U.S. and Chinese Economic Engagement*, GAO-13-199, February 2013.

5 Xinhua, "U.S. Plot to Sow Discord between China, Africa Is Doomed to Fail," August 3, 2012c. Xinhua, "Chinese Envoy Briefs UN on China-Africa Relations," *People's Daily Online*, September 11, 2007. See also Fumbuka Ng'wanakilala and George Obulutsa, "China's Xi Tells Africa He Seeks Relationship of Equals," *Reuters*, March 25, 2013.

6 The best example is perhaps two remarks by then–Secretary of State Hillary Clinton during visits to Africa in 2011 and 2012. See Terry Wing, "Clinton Answers China's Challenge in Africa," Voice of America, August 1, 2012; Reuters, "Clinton Warns against 'New Colonialism' in Africa," June 11, 2011; and *The Guardian*, "Chinese State Media Slam Hillary Clinton's Speech in Africa," August 3, 2012.

continent since the conclusion of the Cold War, and it merits better treatment than such conventional-wisdom approaches.

This report explores the economic, political, and security dimensions of Sino-African relations. Its central conclusion is that China's growing presence in Africa is not a strategic threat to U.S. interests requiring bilateral competition with Beijing. The United States and China share a similar interest in African stability, and Chinese contributions to African development can be positive for both African and American interests. There are areas of natural competition (for market access and diplomatic influence) and areas where American and Chinese interests in Africa contradict, chiefly around democratic governance and adherence to international political norms. However, the issues at stake are generally not zero-sum, and, in any case, are not commensurate with higher levels of political and security competition. Despite this, the climate of strategic distrust between the United States and China threatens to distort and securitize these issues in ways that can damage U.S. ties to both China and African states.

The report begins by exploring the interests driving Chinese relations with African states. It then turns to the behavior and presence generated by these interests, with sections for economic, political, and security relations. It then addresses the potential for change in Chinese interests and behavior over the medium term, and how these dynamics overlap or conflict with American interests. It concludes by addressing the implications for U.S. policymakers.

Historical Antecedents

China's engagement with Africa is not new, though it has changed form and grown substantially since the market-oriented "reform and opening" (改革开放) of the Chinese economy in 1978.[7] Earlier PRC engagement with Africa was strongly ideological and geopolitical, pri-

7 For background on China's "Reform and Opening" movement, see Ezra F. Vogel, *Deng Xiaoping and the Transformation of China*, Cambridge, Mass.: Harvard University Press, Belknap Press, 2011.

marily as an effort to export Maoism, counter American and Soviet influence, and increase China's international influence and reputation.[8] This included doctrines of "third-world solidarity" as well as "moral and material" support to African liberation movements, with Beijing portraying the developing world (including Africa) as split between the forces of socialism and colonialism.[9] Alongside New Delhi, Beijing codified the Five Principles of Peaceful Coexistence in 1954, rhetorically championing an international order marked by noninterference by foreign states in domestic affairs, support for self-determination, and mutual nonaggression.[10]

Alongside the ideology and rhetoric of socialist solidarity, however, geopolitics and national interest shaped China's interaction with African states.[11] Maoist China could be pragmatic at the expense of its ideals, as demonstrated by Beijing's rapprochement with the anticommunist Mobutu Sese Seko in Zaire (now the Democratic Republic of the Congo) while simultaneously supporting Robert Mugabe's

---

[8] For an exceptional history on Sino-African ties, see David H. Shinn and Joshua Eisenman, *China and Africa: A Century of Engagement*, Philadelphia, Pa.: University of Pennsylvania, 2012. For a brief review of Maoist ties with Africa, see Domingos Jardo Muekalia, "Africa and China's Strategic Partnership," *African Security Review*, Vol. 13, No. 1, 2004.

[9] For an excellent review of China's historical and current relations with the developing world, see Joshua Eisenman, Eric Heginbotham, and Derek Mitchell, *China and the Developing World: Beijing's Strategy for the Twenty-First Century*. Armonk, N.Y.: M.E. Sharpe, 2007.

[10] The five principles are commonly cited in People's Republic of China (PRC) discourse concerning foreign policy writ large, and with developing countries in particular. They were recently cited in the April 2013 Defense White Paper as a guiding principle of the PLA's expanding role. The principles are "mutual respect for each other's sovereignty and territorial integrity, mutual non-aggression, non-interference in each other's internal affairs, equality and mutual benefit, and peaceful coexistence" (Information Office of the State Council [IOSC], *The Diversified Employment of China's Armed Forces*, White Paper, Beijing: Ministry of National Defense of the People's Republic of China, April 2013a).

[11] Following the 1955 Bandung Conference, China was notably involved in Angola, the Congo, Algeria, Cameroon, Niger, and the Tutsis in the Rwanda-Burundi conflicts. See David H. Shinn, "Military and Security Relations: China, Africa, and the Rest of the World," in Robert I. Rotberg, ed., *China into Africa: Trade, Aid, and Influence*, Washington, D.C.: Brookings Institution, 2008.

insurgency in Rhodesia (now Zimbabwe).[12] Beijing actively sought to isolate Taiwan's representation in Africa, and African states were instrumental in Beijing's assuming Taipei's seat on the U.N. Security Council in 1971. The rivalry within the communist movement between China and the Soviet Union was expressed by both states competing for influence in Africa against each other as well as against the democratic West.[13] For example, Beijing and Moscow supported opposite sides of the Somali-Ethiopian Ogaden war of the late 1970s, with Beijing providing the Somalis with limited diplomatic support and military assistance.[14] Sino-Soviet tensions also colored Beijing's relations with South Africa, as Beijing shifted support from the African National Congress (ANC) to the Pan-Africanist Congress (PAC) as the ANC positioned itself closer to Moscow. Similarly, Beijing was (and continues to be) a strong supporter of Robert Mugabe's militant Zimbabwe African National Union (ZANU) and its Patriotic Front (ZANU-PF) political movements, opposing for many years both the Western-backed Rhodesian government and other Soviet-backed Marxist militants.[15] South African scholars Victor Ojakorotu and Ayo Whetho concisely summarize the trilateral Cold War competition in Africa: "The West was concerned about Africa's 'romance' with the socialist world just as the Soviets were worried that China's emphasis on revolutionary activity would lead to greater Western interventionism."[16]

Beijing's active involvement in African politics and support for substate liberation movements, while decidedly limited in scope com-

---

[12] I thank Dr. Robert Sutter for this insight. See Shinn and Eisenman, 2012, pp. 74, 291, 339.

[13] Richard J. Payne and Cassandra R. Veney, "China's Post-Cold War African Policy," *Asian Survey*, Vol. 38, No. 9, 1998. For a review of Chinese historical military support to African states, see Shinn and Eisenman, 2012, pp. 162–169.

[14] Roy Lyons, "The USSR, China and the Horn of Africa," *Review of African Political Economy*, Vol. 5, No. 12, 1978.

[15] Douglas Reed, *The Battle for Rhodesia*, Cape Town, South Africa: Haum, 1966.

[16] Victor Ojakorotu and Ayo Whetho, "Sino-African Relations: The Cold War Years and After," *Asia Journal of Global Studies*, Vol. 2, No. 2, 2008.

pared with U.S. and Soviet activity, demonstrates the limits of Beijing's theoretically apolitical approach to Africa. Such activities also stand at odds with the PRC's current interpretation of the Five Principles' emphasis on strict noninterference in the affairs of other states. In comparison to political activity, early twentieth-century Sino-African economic interaction was decidedly limited; Sino-African annual trade in 1950 stood at $12 million, rising to a still relatively small $100 million by 1960. China did provide some selected assistance to African development, most notably by sending engineers and laborers to help construct the Tanzania-Zambia railroad, as well as sending doctors to African states since the early 1960s.[17]

Chinese economic interests, however, have gradually subsumed Beijing's previous ideological and political interests as drivers of Chinese behavior in Africa. Beginning with the fallout from the Great Leap Forward and Cultural Revolution, continuing with the closing of the Cold War, and accelerating alongside China's economic development, China's political interests in Africa have waned relative to growing economic ties. The ascendency of China's economic interests is reflected in a stream of economic and political events over the past three decades: China becoming an oil importer in 1993; Chinese Communist Party (CCP) reorganization and packaging of aid, trade, and investment to Africa in the mid-1990s; admission to the World Trade Organization (WTO) in 2001; and roughly an order of magnitude expansion of economic ties over the past ten years. In contrast to its earlier incarnations, current Chinese engagement with African states is nonideological; Beijing engages readily with democratic, authoritarian, and theocratic regimes alike. As expressed in China's 2006, 2010, and 2013 White Papers on Sino-African ties, this engagement is premised

---

[17] China continues to send doctors to African states. For an exceptional review of Chinese engagement with Africa and Chinese aid, see Deborah Brautigam, *The Dragon's Gift: The Real Story of China in Africa*, Oxford: Oxford University Press, 2009. For medical teams, see pp. 117–119 and 316–320.

on eschewing political considerations to seek mutual benefit.[18] In so doing, Beijing has continued to quote the Five Principles as a cornerstone of its African relations.

---

[18] Note that Beijing's 2006 White Paper on policy in Africa (People's Republic of China, *China's African Policy*, Beijing, January 12, 2006) covers Sino-African relations broadly, while the 2006 (IOSC, *China's National Defense in 2006*, White Paper, Beijing: Ministry of National Defense of the People's Republic of China, 2006), 2010 (IOSC, *China's National Defense in 2010*, White Paper, Beijing: Ministry of National Defense of the People's Republic of China, 2010), and 2013 (IOSC, 2013a) CCP White Papers focus more narrowly on economic and trade issues.

CHAPTER TWO

China's African Interests and Strategic Perceptions

This chapter describes the strategic interests and perceptions driving Chinese behavior in Africa. This description considers the range of economic, political, and security interests across the relevant Chinese government, commercial, and military stakeholders. Such interests can be in tension with one another—for example, Beijing's interest in market access versus its desire for a favorable international image. More importantly, Beijing's interest in the stability of its trading partners and protecting overseas investments has gradually grown over the past decade despite being in tension with Beijing's interests in promoting international norms of nonintervention and absolute sovereignty. As noted in Chapter One, such interests have been in flux throughout the twentieth century, and China's African relationships continue to exhibit complexity and change. How China's key stakeholders weigh these competing interests as Sino-African relationships continue to evolve will naturally shape China's future behavior.

Economic Interests: Natural Resources and Market Access

China's government and commercial actors see in Africa a source for natural resource imports, a growing and relatively underutilized market for exports and investment, and an opportunity for Chinese firms to gain experience and increase domestic employment. In China's case, the pressure for economic growth is highlighted by the perceived links between economic performance, social stability, and continued CCP rule.[1] China's investment in Africa also occurs in the broader context of Beijing's "Go Global" (走出去) commercial strategy, intended to increase outgoing Chinese investment and commercial presence.[2]

Sino-African economic relationships often have strong structural roots. Africa is well positioned to contribute to China's growing resource demand; the continent has more than 10 percent of global oil reserves and 7.5 percent of global natural gas reserves (with upside potential in both, given the relative lack of exploration), and a strong resource base in high-demand minerals and metals.[3] To realize the development of these resources, many African states seek affordable foreign investment capital and infrastructure development, relative strong suits for Chinese firms.[4]

It is therefore unsurprising that natural resource imports constitute China's, as well as the United States' and other industrialized states', most important economic interest in Africa. Oil is particularly important; China seeks both greater supply and greater diversity of suppliers in the context of rapid demand growth and plateauing

---

[1] Susan L. Shirk, *China: Fragile Superpower*, Oxford: Oxford University Press, 2007.

[2] The "Go Global" policy was outlined in the CCP's tenth Five-Year Plan in 2001 (China Internet Information Center, "China Mapping Out the 11th Five-Year Development Guidelines," website, China.org, undated), and reaffirmed in the 12th Five-Year Plan in 2011 (People's Republic of China, *Twelfth Five-Year Plan*, trans. Delegation of the European Union in China, March 2011). The policy calls for Chinese firms and institutions to expand China's outgoing foreign direct investment (FDI) globally and to place an equal importance on outgoing and incoming FDI. Doing so facilitates several goals, among them the ownership of assets abroad, a larger global role for Chinese finance, the development of "national champion" firms, and expanding overseas markets for Chinese exports. See Linda Yueh, "China's 'Going Out, Bringing In' Policy: the Geo-economics of China's Rise," International Institute of Strategic Studies Geo-Economics and Strategy Seminar, *A New Era of Geo-Economics: Assessing the Interplay of Economic and Political Risk*, March 25, 2012.

[3] See Charles Roxburgh, Norbert Dörr, Acha Leke, Amine Tazi-Riffi, Arend van Wamelen, Susan Lund, Mutsa Chironga, Tarik Alatovik, Charles Atkins, Nadia Terfous, and Till Zeino-Mahmalat, *Lions on the Move: The Progress and Potential of African Economies*, McKinsey Global Institute, June 2010, pp. 2, 39–46. For natural gas, see Ernst & Young Global Limited, *Natural Gas in Africa: The Frontiers of the Golden Age*, 2012, p. 6.

[4] Roxburgh et al., 2010, pp. 39–46.

domestic production.[5] Because China remained an oil exporter as late as 1993 and expected further self-sufficiency for at least several years hence, Chinese firms are relative late-comers to the international oil game. As such, despite explosive import growth, Chinese firms lack the market penetration and experience of major international oil firms, and China's energy regulation sector remains relatively nascent.[6] China is currently the world's second-largest oil consumer and importer (behind the United States on both counts), consuming 10.2 million barrels per day (mbpd), of which around 5.6 mbpd is imported.[7] Dramatic import demand growth is expected to continue; mainstream sources project China will domestically produce only a quarter of its oil consumption by 2035, requiring around 13 mbpd in imports.[8] China currently receives more than two-thirds of its imported oil from the Middle East and Africa: 2.6 mbpd from the Middle East (about 46 percent of imports) and 1.2 mbpd from Africa (21 percent of imports). The plateauing of Asian conventional oil field production, combined with rising demand, will likely further consolidate China's imports on the Middle East, concentrating China's supply chain and, in turn, reducing national energy security.[9] This highlights the longer-term energy security value of African oil relationships for both oil supply and diversity. In addition, Africa has a stronger market share of several key min-

---

5 Energy security is generally enhanced by supply diversification. Concentration of resource supply in a small group of sources raises the risks and costs of an individual disruption. See Daniel Yergin, "Ensuring Energy Security," *Foreign Affairs*, Vol. 85, No. 2, March/April 2006.

6 Erica Downs, "Who's Afraid of China's Oil Companies?" in Carlos Pascual and Jonathan Elkind, eds., *Energy Security: Economics, Politics, Strategy, and Implications*, Washington, D.C.: Brookings Institution, 2009. See also Erica Downs, "China's 'New' Energy Administration," *China Business Review*, November 2008.

7 U.S. Energy Information Administration, *China Country Analysis Brief*, Washington, D.C.: U.S. Department of Energy, April 22, 2013a.

8 International Energy Agency, *World Energy Outlook 2012*, Paris, November 12, 2012.

9 International Energy Agency, 2012; see also Andrew Erickson and Gabe Collins, "China's Oil Security Pipe Dream," *Naval War College Review*, Vol. 63, No. 2, 2010.

erals than it has in the global oil market, several of which are key Chinese economic inputs.[10]

A rather exclusive focus on natural resource imports can distract Western observers from China's other major economic interest in Africa: access to African markets for exports, investments, employment, and experience. While the disparity has narrowed over the past several years, the past decade has seen China import significantly less African oil than the United States and European Union and have far more balanced trade with African states.[11] Further underscoring the value of African economic relations are the slow recovery of developed world economies and continuing pressure on Beijing to support firm performance and generate employment. African states, with a growing population of more than 1 billion, have an aggregate gross domestic product (GDP) of $1.6 trillion—roughly equivalent to Russia or Brazil.[12] Contemporary Africa is nearly as urbanized as China and has as many cities of 1 million people or greater as Europe.[13] The continent has been averaging 4.5 percent annual GDP growth since 2000. Experts project continued growth (aggregate African GDP is expected to grow by an additional $1 trillion by 2020), with a young popula-

---

[10] Particularly iron, manganese, cobalt, and copper, and potentially cotton diamonds, bauxite, gold, and chromium and platinum group metals. See Charles Roxburgh et al., 2010, p. 2, pp. 39–46. See also W. David Menzie, "China's Quest for Resources," testimony before the U.S.-China Economic and Security Review Commission hearing on "China's Global Quest for Resources and Implications for the United States," January 26, 2012; U.S. Geological Survey (USGS), *2012 Minerals Yearbook: China*, U.S. Department of the Interior, December 2013; and USGS, *2012 Minerals Yearbook: Africa Summary*, U.S. Department of the Interior, December 2014.

[11] IMF, undated; United Nations, undated(a); and UNCTAD, undated(a). The shale boom in the United States may adjust this balance. However, even accounting for the growth in Chinese oil demand, China remained roughly 600,000 barrels per day below the United States in consuming African oil in 2011. See U.S. Energy Information Administration, "Overview Data for China," web page, May 30, 2013b; and U.S. Energy Information Administration, "Overview Data for United States," web page, May 30, 2013c.

[12] Brown, 2012, p. 23.

[13] Roxburgh et al., 2010, p. 16.

tion that is urbanizing and gaining purchasing power.[14] Africa's corresponding growth in incoming FDI has also been strong—increasing from $9 billion annually in 2000 to $62 billion in 2008.[15]

Of Brazil, Russia, India, and China (or *BRIC countries*), China is leading a broader trend of investing in Africa. The world's developing economies now account for nearly half (46 percent) of Africa's trade.[16] To paraphrase the U.S. National Defense University's David Brown, Chinese actors tend to view Africa through an "optimist" lens, while Western actors' focus on famine and conflict has generated a "pessimistic" perspective.[17] Investments in Africa are often of the higher-risk and higher-yield variety; China's appetite for investment opportunities, relatively young Chinese firms, and large currency reserves encourage participation. In particular, Chinese construction, engineering, and resource firms have sought to expand into African markets. These markets provide Chinese firms with opportunities to develop key overseas experience, in a broader context of China attempting to build "national champion" firms that can compete in international business.[18] As part

---

[14] Peter Pham, "Assessing China's Role and Influence in Africa," testimony before the Committee of Foreign Affairs hearing for the Subcommittee on Africa, Global Health, and Human Rights, March 29, 2012. Also, Roxburgh et al., 2010, p. 3.

[15] Roxburgh et al., 2010, p. 3.

[16] Depending on the estimate, the number is around 46 percent. This has been part of a broader "south-south" economic interaction, driven by both developing world growth and the 2008 financial crisis, which hit developed world sources of capital and trade harder than developing ones. See Roxburgh et al., 2010, p. 2, pp. 39–46. See also *The Economist*, 2013. For individual country data, see IMF, undated.

[17] Brown, 2012, p. iv.

[18] These are similar in some ways to Japanese *keiretsu* and Korean *chaebol*. Funding goes to Chinese corporate behemoths that dominate strategic sectors in the Chinese economy itself, some of which are likely intended—at least by the PRC government's national planning agency, the National Development Reform Council—for Fortune 500 status. Client firms include the national oil corporations China National Offshore Oil Corporation, China National Petroleum Corporation, and China Petroleum & Chemical Corporation (Sinopec); telecom firms Huawei and ZTE Corporation; and construction firms China Harbour, China State Construction Engineering Corporation, and China National Electronics Import and Export Corporation. See Li-Wen Lin and Curtis Milhaupt, "We Are the (National) Champions: Understanding the Mechanisms of State Capitalism in China," *Stanford Law Review*, Vol. 65, 2013.

of wider economic rebalancing, Beijing also seeks to transition dangerous, environmentally hazardous, and low-skill industries to overseas operations, including in Africa.[19]

Political Interests: Influence, Stability, and Favorable Precedents

While they are less critical than its economic interests, Beijing's four primary political interests in Africa are bolstering China's international image and influence, isolating Taiwan, countering problematic international norms, and supporting the stability of economic partners.

With regard to China's image and influence, Beijing has gone to great lengths to emphasize the peaceful rise of Chinese power. Successful Sino-African relations are beneficial to this effort. Continuing the Cold War context of third-world solidarity, Beijing's rhetoric often features a selective reading of the West's colonial past to present China as an alternative to imperialism, colonialism, and great-power politics. While China has never publicly claimed to foster an alternative development model (though occasionally extolling its virtues in books published by CCP publishers[20]), support for a loosely defined "Beijing Consensus" of state-based capitalism and tighter political control can increase both Beijing's prestige and the legitimacy of the CCP's continued domestic political and economic centralization.[21]

Beijing likely sees several opportunities to translate increased influence with African states into tangible diplomatic benefits. African states have three seats on the U.N. Security Council and constitute more than one-quarter of U.N. General Assembly votes. Such votes

---

19 Brautigam, 2009, pp. 90–93.

20 Wei Pan, *Zhongguo Mo Shi: Jie Du Renmin Gongheguo De 60 Nian* [*China Model: A New Developmental Model from the 60 Years of the People's Republic*], Beijing: Zhong Yang Bian Yi Chu Ban She, 2009.

21 While the "Beijing Consensus" is a Western term, Chinese sources do portray parts of China's state-led economic model as an alternative to that of the more private-led model of Western states. For example, Xinhua, "China's Development Model Good Example for African Nations: CCM Vice-Chairman of Tanzania," June 21, 2012a.

can be diplomatically valuable; for example, African states were central to the PRC's accession to the U.N. Security Council in the early 1970s. Beijing frequently recounts this support in its relations with African states.[22] Beijing would like similar African support on the U.N. Human Rights Council, which occasionally criticizes Chinese practices, as well as African support within the WTO.[23] Finally, while diplomatic competition with Taiwan is relatively dormant at present, China has a continuing interest in politically isolating Taipei. With Gambia's November 2013 severing of diplomatic ties with Taipei, Taiwan is recognized in Africa by only three states: Swaziland, Burkina Faso, and Sao Tome and Principe.[24]

With regard to international norms, African support can also assist Beijing in countering precedents that it views as potentially dangerous domestically. In both a legal and diplomatic perspective, Beijing likely perceives an interest in preventing an active international consensus on a host of domestic issues: civil society and human rights, democratic representation, independence of judiciary, and transparency of government. China's stance of noninterference in domestic governance and human rights issues is often appreciated and reciprocated by African governments, even among those with democratic traditions and solid human rights practices.[25] African states have generally been silent, with some making supportive statements, during several periods of increased scrutiny of CCP human rights, including the 1989 Tiananmen massacre and 2008 Tibetan riots.[26]

Finally, Beijing has a growing interest in African stability, commensurate with its growing economic and political investment therein. African stability benefits Chinese actors in several ways. China's grow-

---

[22] David H. Shinn, "The Impact of China's Growing Influence in Africa," *The European Financial Review*, April 2011a, p. 16.

[23] Shinn, 2011a, p. 17.

[24] Note that as of January 2015, Beijing had not officially recognized ties with Gambia. See BBC, "Gambia Severs Diplomatic Ties with Taiwan," November 15, 2013; and Joel Atkinson, "Gambia's Break with Taiwan," *The Diplomat*, December 2, 2013.

[25] Shinn, 2011a, p. 16.

[26] Brown, 2012, p. 8.

ing human and economic investment in African states, and desire for African natural resource supply and diversification, incentivize a growing interest in African stability.[27] The most obvious targets for such attention at present are limited to China's direct trading and investment partners; consider, for example, China's recent role in mediating conflict between the two Sudans and between rival factions in South Sudan.[28] As Sino-African economic links grow, and particularly if African sources of raw materials become more critical to supply diversification, Beijing's interest in the stability of partner states can be expected to grow. Further, given the degree to which violence in Africa can transcend national borders, a broader focus beyond resource partners may emerge over the medium term. Undermining African stability, or being perceived as doing so, also damages China's international image. Beijing has responded, albeit belatedly, to Western pressure over human rights issues (in Sudan, for example) and has shown a preference for not being the only foreign power opposing international consensus on intervention issues.[29]

Security Interests: Answering Emerging and Awkward Challenges

China's emerging security interests in Africa are driven by, and subordinate to, Beijing's larger goals of safeguarding economic development and increasing political influence. As a regional power with expanding global interests, China is in the process of defining its security practices, missions, and presence in some of the world's most unstable

[27] Ely Ratner, "The Emergent Security Threats Reshaping China's Rise," *The Washington Quarterly*, Vol. 34, No. 1, 2011.

[28] Jacey Fortin, "China in the Middle: South Sudan's Biggest Oil Importer Learns to Wield Its Clout," *International Business Times*, April 9, 2014.

[29] See Evan S. Medeiros, *China's International Behavior: Activism, Opportunism, and Diversification*, Santa Monica, Calif.: RAND Corporation, MG-850-AF, 2009, pp. 173–194.

areas.[30] China likely has more than 15,000 overseas enterprises (including more than 2,000 in Africa[31]) with well more than 1 million overseas citizens.[32] Chinese firms have active investments and contracts of more than $1 billion in 12 of the top 20 global failed or failing states.[33] China now confronts security threats in Africa that many Western states and firms have long faced. The explosion of Chinese economic interests, assets, and citizens in Africa over the past ten years, however, has outpaced China's ability to secure them. This generates an emerging set of security interests that has yet to be fully defined.

Beijing's foremost emerging security interest is protecting the growing number of citizens and assets from internal instability, terrorism, and kidnapping.[34] This has recently included, in a nascent sense, two of the PLA's highest-profile overseas operations: securing Chinese merchant traffic from piracy near the Horn of Africa and evacuating large numbers of Chinese citizens from Libya in 2011. With regard to terrorism, due in part to Islamist misgivings about China's treatment of its domestic Muslim Uighur population, al Qaeda in the Islamic Maghreb and Nigerian militants have pledged attacks against Chinese businesses in Africa.[35] Kidnappings of Chinese workers have already proven problematic in several areas of Africa, with at least 13 kidnapping incidents in the past five years.[36] Providing adequate security for

---

[30] For background on China's evolving perceptions on security, see Andrew J. Nathan and Andrew Scobell, *China's Search for Security*, New York: Columbia University Press, 2012.; and James C. Mulvenon, "Chairman Hu and the PLA's 'New Historic Missions,'" *China Leadership Monitor*, 2009.

[31] Deborah Brautigam, "Chinese Investment in Africa: How Much?" *China in Africa: The Real Story*, blog post, September 28, 2013b.

[32] Zhang Haizhou, "Protection of Overseas Chinese Citizens and Assets Proposed," *China Daily*, March 9, 2012.

[33] The most comprehensive and accurate data on Chinese global investments is The Heritage Foundation and American Enterprise Institute, "China Global Investment Tracker," Washington, D.C., 2012.

[34] Ratner, 2011, pp. 29–44.

[35] Ratner, 2011, pp. 31–32.

[36] Peter Ford, "Why Chinese Workers Are Getting Kidnapped Abroad," *Christian Science Monitor*, February 1, 2012.

its citizens and assets guards against several difficult outcomes: a loss of domestic political legitimacy stemming from an inability to protect Chinese citizens, Chinese commercial actors being dissuaded from investing or doing business in Africa, and scenarios (internal conflicts, kidnappings, or terrorist attacks) in which Beijing is forced to intervene politically or militarily.

Beijing's remaining security interests in Africa are to buoy its reputation as a global leader and increase the experience of the PLA. Beijing has identified a role for the PLA in providing security and assistance on the global stage.[37] As such, Chinese security participation in Africa supports China's broader interest in portraying a peaceful rise, as well as Sino-African solidarity. The most obvious example of this is widespread Chinese participation in U.N. peacekeeping forces in Africa. This showcases China's commitment to great-power responsibilities and benevolent intent. Such deployments also generate operational experience for the PLA (particularly the Army), which last saw actual combat in 1979 with a lackluster performance during China's incursions into Vietnam. Such experience and attention is likely of particular importance to the PLA Ground Force, which has traditionally been at the forefront of PLA leadership but is under pressure, given the current air- and maritime-focused Chinese security climate.[38] The deployment of the PLA Navy (PLAN)'s hospital ship and search and rescue capabilities also contributes to Beijing's international and Africa-specific public diplomacy interests.

To date, Beijing has taken remarkably little interest in directly exporting security. This likely stems from three factors: the PLA's current limitations in power projection,[39] a reflexive fear of international

---

[37] To quote President Hu's 2004 speech on "New Historic Missions," "China plays an important role in safeguarding world peace. . . . It provides humanitarian aid and dispatches rescue teams to countries hit by severe natural disasters" (Mulvenon, 2009).

[38] It is worth noting, however, that U.N. deployments do not greatly benefit the PLA's operational experience in expeditionary warfare, because most of the expeditionary logistics are handled by the United Nations.

[39] The PLA does not currently have the capacity, operational capabilities, logistical support, overseas diplomatic and material arrangements, or operational experience to support large-scale power projection activity. See Office of the Secretary of Defense, *Annual Report*

perceptions of China as a threat, and Beijing's diplomatic commitment to not intervening in the affairs of other states. Rather, the PRC's Ministry of Foreign Affairs has managed most of the security issues related to Chinese citizens in Africa. How directly Beijing addresses these emerging threats may change as China's overseas interests and PLA capability continue to grow. Beijing has an interest in the stability of the countries in which it has a significant footprint of citizens and investments, and such an interest can naturally lead to exporting more security to assure stability. While PLA capabilities to do so are limited at present, the PLA's role has grown both doctrinally in the CCP articulation on the PLA's global missions and operationally in PLA activity on the continent. Both are likely to continue to evolve alongside the increasing investments of people and capital shaping Beijing's security interests.[40]

to Congress: Military and Security Developments Involving the People's Republic of China 2014, U.S. Department of Defense, April 24, 2014.

[40] Ratner, 2011.

CHAPTER THREE

Chinese Presence and Behavior in Africa

This chapter describes the behavior of Chinese economic, political, and military actors in Africa, driven by the interests described in Chapter Two. This review includes particular attention on natural resource imports, arms exports, loans and investments, political engagement, and military activities. The chapter concludes by considering near- and medium-term changes to Sino-African relations.

Sino-African Economic Relations

In both trade and investment, Sino-African economic relations have expanded dramatically in the past ten years. These ties have elevated Africa from minimal to moderate economic significance for China and have made China a key variable in several African economies. While there is legitimate disagreement about the extent to which China's growing influence has undercut political norms and supported problematic regimes (see this report's conclusions in Chapter Four), China's increasing trade and investment has clearly contributed greatly to African economic growth, particularly in infrastructure development.[1]

Three points must be highlighted before any exploration of Sino-African economic relations. First, comprehensive and reliable data are difficult to acquire, particularly in capital flows.[2] Given areas of

[1] Deborah Brautigam, "Africa's Eastern Promise," *Foreign Affairs*, January 2010a.

[2] Deborah Brautigam, "China in Africa: Really Rubbery Numbers," *China in Africa: The Real Story*, blog post, March 30, 2013a.

low regulation, black markets, routing of investment through Hong Kong or overseas tax shelters, speed and volume of private transactions, and transparency issues, much of the data are suggestive rather than authoritative. Second, economic statistics taken out of context can be misleading. African GDP and bilateral trade growth have been buoyed by increasing global commodity prices. An analysis of the value of bilateral trade growth out of context suggests more-robust growth in trade volume than has occurred. In addition, trade with Africa is growing globally, not just with China. For example, American trade with Africa increased threefold between 2000 and 2010, from $39 billion to $113 billion, compared with China's nearly twentyfold growth, from less than $10 billion in 2000 to more than $180 billion in 2012.[3]

Interestingly, and relatively underreported, the growth in China's trade has not displaced the role of developed states but instead has tended to capitalize on African growth.[4] Put differently, rather than replacing previous trade between African and Western states, the growth in Sino-African trade has generated new trade, particularly new contracts for African exports and new demand for Chinese construction and manufactured goods. Further, with some exceptions, the United States and China tend to operate in different industries and sectors in Africa rather than be in direct competition.[5] In general, Western firms are stronger in the more expensive and high technology sectors, while Chinese firms are stronger in lower-end technology.[6] For example, Western firms have a far stronger position in exports of aircraft and in African states' energy sectors, while Chinese firms are stronger in exports of most consumer goods.[7] China's investment growth in Africa is a small piece of the wider "Go Global" investment effort, rather than

---

[3] Brown, 2012, p. 15.

[4] Brown, 2012, p. 11.

[5] GAO, 2013.

[6] GAO, 2013.

[7] GAO, 2013; Bo Kong, *China's International Petroleum Policy*, Santa Barbara, Calif.: Praeger Security International, 2009.

a specific targeting of Africa.[8] Finally, there is no single Sino-African economic relationship, and interactions vary widely across states and substate communities. As discussed next, there are also a range of Chinese economic actors in Africa, often pursuing disparate ends.

Chinese Economic Actors in Africa

Chinese commercial actors can be loosely grouped into three categories: large, state-owned enterprises (SOEs) pursuing infrastructure and resource projects; large-to-medium private interests pursuing a range of markets; and small, private merchants farming or selling within African marketplaces.[9] In terms of value, state-owned firms have been by far the most active in Africa, though private-firm activity is expanding. Contrary to the image of a monolithic central government commanding subordinate firms for geopolitical gain, Beijing has struggled to exert control over the large number of foreign-trading companies.[10] Even in the case of SOEs, a large body of research attests their balancing of party and profit motives and operational autonomy from Beijing's control.[11] Private actors, or those owned by Chinese local governments, are more difficult to direct; in general, the smaller and more private a firm, the less control Beijing is likely to have.[12] Liberalization

---

[8] From 2003 to 2013, China's global outgoing FDI increased more than thirtyfold. This, however, occurred from a small initial base of outgoing FDI. According to UNCTAD's most recent statistics, as of 2013, China was the third-largest contributor of outgoing FDI, behind the United States and Japan. For UNCTAD statistics, see UNCTAD, "UNCTADstat," web tool, undated(b); for further background on China's "Go Global" investment, see Yueh, 2012.

[9] David H. Shinn and Kerry Brown, *Africa Programme Meeting Summary—China and Africa: A Century of Engagement*, Chatham House, June 29, 2012, p. 3.

[10] See Kenneth Lieberthal and David M. Lampton, *Bureaucracy, Politics, and Decision Making in Post-Mao China*, Berkeley, Calif.: University of California Press, 1992. For a more contemporary update on Lieberthal's seminal work, see Andrew Mertha, "Fragmented Authoritarianism 2.0: Political Pluralization in the Chinese Policy Process," *The China Quarterly*, Vol. 220, 2009.

[11] Many of the interests of profit-driven firms and the CCP overlap, but not all. See Lieberthal and Lampton, 1992; and Mertha, 2009. For the oil industry in particular, see Downs, 2008.

[12] Chen Zhimin and Jian Junbo, *Chinese Provinces as Foreign Policy Actors*, South African Institute of International Affairs, January 2012.

of the Chinese economy exacerbated this problem, creating thousands of smaller corporations conducting foreign trade. While private actors have generally created value for African states,[13] they can also leverage their relative freedom from Beijing to engage in corruption and to skirt labor, trademark, and environmental standards.[14] Beijing has tried to more effectively regulate private actors, though this is difficult, given the distances involved and weak oversight mechanisms of the CCP and many host governments.[15]

Sino-African Trade

Even by the standards of Chinese and African GDP and aggregate trade growth, the volume of Sino-African trade has grown enormously since 2000, at an annual rate of nearly 16 percent.[16] While there is some discrepancy among sources,[17] according to the IMF Direction of Trade Statistics database, in 2012, total Sino-African trade reached $180 billion—$105.4 billion (59 percent) in Chinese imports from Africa and $74.6 billion (41 percent) in African imports from China. In that year, Sino-African trade grew more than 19 percent, with growth in exports to China (21 percent) significantly outpacing Chinese exports to Africa (17 percent).[18]

While no state is in a position to monopolize Africa's trade, China has risen to be the single largest state for both imports to and exports

---

13 Brautigam, 2009.

14 In the most extreme cases, this includes quasi-legal business syndicates (such as the Queensway Group that controls much of Angola's oil exports) and Chinese organized crime. See Brown, 2012, p. 67.

15 Brown, 2012, p. 68.

16 IOSC, *China-Africa Economic and Trade Cooperation 2013*, White Paper, Beijing, August 2013b.

17 Sources include IMF, undated; UNCTAD, undated(a); and Chinese government statistics. Data on Sino-African trade and finance varies significantly depending on the source. As noted, reporting and transparency issues mean that such statistics are suggestive rather than definitive. Further, as of December 2013, there is a discrepancy with the IMF data set concerning Chinese imports from Africa: Africa's data set shows $60.43 billion of exports to China, while China's data set shows $105.4 billion in imports from Africa.

18 Data compiled from IMF, undated; see IOSC, 2013b.

from African states (though it is second to the aggregated European Union in both). China had risen as a market for African exports from around 1 percent in 1995 to more than 15 percent in 2012. The United States is the third–most prevalent destination, with around 8 percent.[19] For exports to Africa, China's share has increased ninefold since 2000 (including a 21 percent rise in 2012), giving it a share of nearly 15 percent.[20] This compares with about 30 percent for the European Union as a whole, and 6 percent for the United States. China's export strength has given it more balanced trade with Africa as a whole than the United States or European Union for much of the past decade. However, since 2010, African exports to China have been rising at a faster pace than Chinese exports to Africa, and China's current trade deficit with Africa ($30.8 billion) stands between those of the United States ($36 billion) and the European Union ($23 billion).

Sino-African trade relations are generally of less value to China's economy than to the economies of African states. For many African states, particularly in sub-Saharan Africa, trade with China is important to national economic health (see Table 3.1). Sino-African trade accounted for 15 percent of the continent's total trade in 2012, up from about 4 percent in 2000.[21] Sub-Saharan Africa has seen the greatest effect, with Chinese sources rising from below 1 percent of sub-Saharan African trade in 1990 to an approximately 17 percent share by 2010.[22] Yet African states together still accounted for only 5.1 percent of China's total trade in 2012 (about the same as Germany), up from 2.2 percent in 2000.[23] China's largest African trading partner is South Africa, constituting about 1.5 percent of China's annual trade, followed by Angola at about 1 percent and Nigeria at around a quarter of a percent. If Chinese trade with African partners is aggregated,

---

19 Derived from IMF, undated.

20 Trade data derived from IMF, undated. On the ninefold rise, see Shinn and Brown, 2012. On growth rate, see IOSC, 2013b.

21 Derived from IMF, undated.

22 Derived from IMF, undated.

23 Brown, 2012, p. 15.

Table 3.1
China's Leading Trade Partners in Africa

Rank	State	2012 Total Chinese Trade ($ millions)	2012 Total Sino-African Trade (%)	2012 Chinese Imports ($ millions)	2012 Chinese Imports from Africa (%)	2012 Chinese Exports ($ millions)	2012 Chinese Exports to Africa (%)	2012 Chinese Trade Balance ($ millions)
1	South Africa	59,949.8	33	44,615.5	42	15,334.4	21	–29,281.1
2	Angola	37,502.5	21	33,458.3	32	4,044.2	5	–29,414.2
3	Nigeria	10,573.8	6	1,266.2	1	9,307.6	12	8,041.4
4	Egypt	9,546.4	5	1,321.4	1	8,225.0	11	6,903.5
5	Libya	8,760.3	5	6,368.2	6	2,392.1	3	–3,976.1
6	Algeria	7,737.4	4	2,319.8	2	5,417.6	7	3,097.8
7	Ghana	5,432.3	3	642.8	1	4,789.5	6	4,146.7
8	Congo, Republic of the	5,075.7	3	4,555.0	4	520.7	1	–4,034.3
9	Congo, Democratic Republic of the	4,347.1	2	3,508.8	3	838.4	1	–2,670.4
10	Sudan	4,220.4	2	2,040.3	2	2,180.1	3	139.8
11	Morocco	3,692.2	2	562.2	1	3,130.0	4	2,567.8
12	Togo	3,468.5	2	84.8	0	3,383.8	5	3,299.0
13	Zambia	3,384.7	2	2,688.6	3	696.2	1	–1,992.4
14	Kenya	2,841.1	2	52.3	0	2,788.8	4	2,736.5
15	Benin	2,675.4	1	261.7	0	2,413.6	3	2,151.9
	All other African states	10,745.6	6	1,651.4	2	9,094.1	12	7,442.7

SOURCE: Data derived from IMF, undated.

NOTE: Some percentage columns may not add to 100 due to rounding.

China's $105.4 billion in 2012 imports from Africa would make the continent China's sixth-largest import source, at 5.8 percent, between the United States (7.1 percent) and Germany (5.1 percent). Similarly, if aggregated, Africa would be China's sixth-largest export market, at 3.6 percent ($74.6 billion), between South Korea (4.3 percent) and Germany (3.4 percent), but far less than the United States (China's leading export market at more than 17 percent).[24] However, Sino-African trade has grown at a faster pace than trade with other regions. While China's global trade increased eightfold from 2000 to 2010, its trade with Africa increased elevenfold.[25] South Africa is China's most important economic relationship in Africa, constituting more than one-third of Sino-African trade and the leading destination for Chinese FDI.

Similar to the United States and the European Union, about 90 percent of China's imports from Africa consist of natural resources (these imports are explored in further depth in the following section).[26] In 2012, 84 percent of China's imports came from four states, with South Africa and Angola alone accounting for almost 75 percent (see Figure 3.1). Given the dominance of natural resources in African exports, African states' trade balances with China vary widely; 15 resource-exporting states tend to run trade surpluses, while more than 30 African states that do not have attractive resources generally run trade deficits, some of which are significant.[27] Mauritius, for example, imported $433 million of goods and services from Chinese firms in 2010, while exporting only $10 million to Chinese consumers.[28]

---

[24] Derived from IMF, undated.

[25] Brown, 2012, p. 15.

[26] Shinn, 2011a, p 17. According to IMF 2012 Direction of Trade Statistics (IMF, undated), South Africa contributed 42.3 percent; Angola, 31.7 percent; Libya, 6 percent; and Republic of the Congo, 4.3 percent. Algeria, the Democratic Republic of the Congo (DRC), Sudan, and Zambia all contributed around 2 percent.

[27] IMF, undated. See also Shinn, 2011a. For example, in 2012, Ghana ran a $4.1 billion deficit, Zimbabwe and Cameroon had relatively balanced trade, and Angola had nearly $30 billion surpluses.

[28] Shinn and Eisenman, 2012, p. 279.

Figure 3.1
Share of Annual Sino-African Trade, by African State, 2012

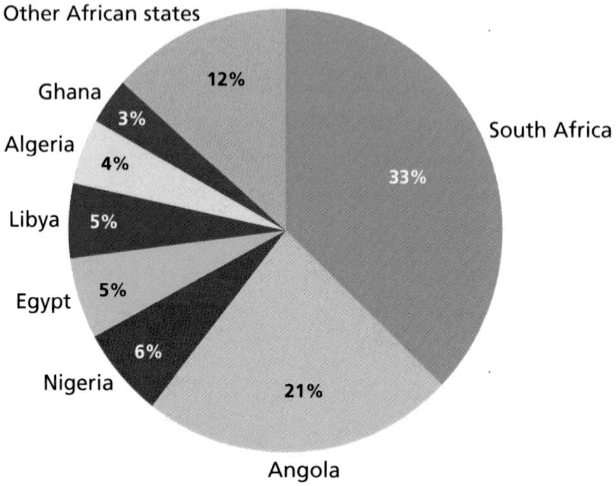

RAND *RR905-3.1*

Beijing has attempted to address these imbalances through a range of measures, including encouraging the consumption of African goods, but efforts have met with little or mixed results.[29]

Chinese exports to African states are more widely distributed than its imports (Figure 3.2 and Figure 3.3). The top eight countries account for 72 percent of export value, with South Africa, Nigeria, and Egypt constituting nearly half (44 percent).[30] Chinese exports are well-suited to African demand, because Chinese consumer goods and services are generally less expensive than those of other foreign competitors. China's domestic development has driven construction, engineering, and machinery sectors that are well positioned to compete

[29] African Center for Economic Transformation, *Looking East: China-Africa Engagements—Ghana Country Case Study*, Accra, Ghana, December 2009, p. 5; Gao Wenzhi, "Work by Mutual Efforts to Promote Trade and Economic Collaboration Between Ghana and China," remarks to Standard Chartered Bank professional forum, Accra, Ghana, October 1, 2013.

[30] Derived from IMF, undated: South Africa, 20.6 percent; Nigeria, 12.5 percent; Egypt, 11 percent; Algeria, 7.4 percent; Ghana, 6.4 percent; and Angola, 5.4 percent. Eight states have between 2 and 5 percent.

Figure 3.2
Share of Annual Chinese Exports to Africa, by African State, 2012

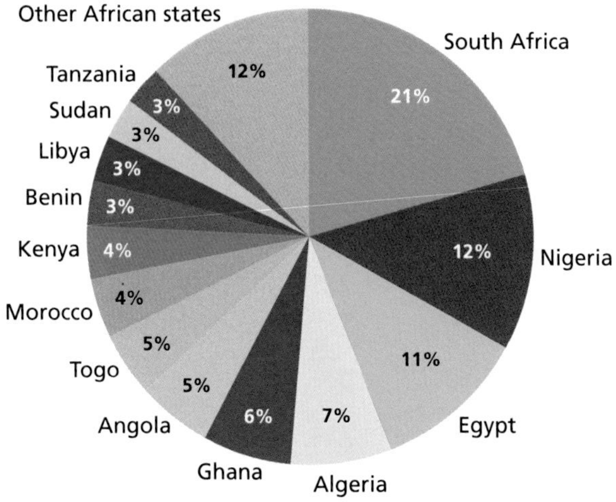

RAND *RR905-3.2*

Figure 3.3
Share of Annual Chinese Imports from Africa, by African State, 2012

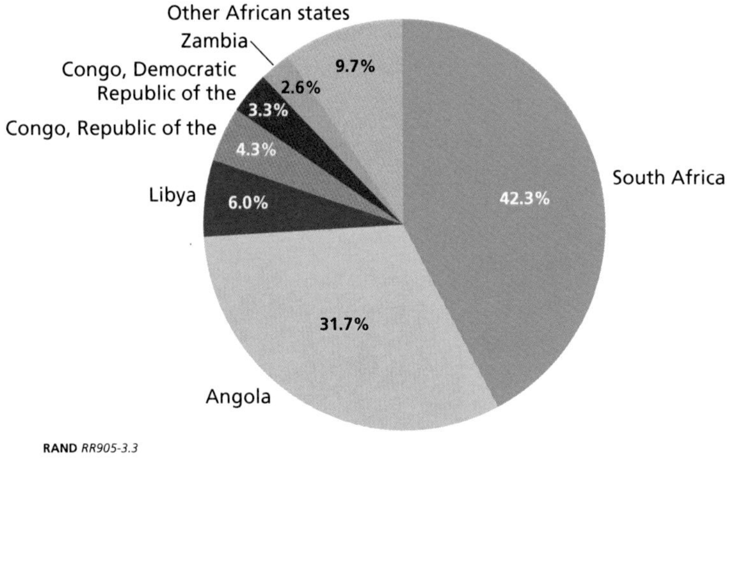

RAND *RR905-3.3*

for similar infrastructure projects in Africa. At around $40 billion in contracts during 2012, Africa is the second-largest overseas market for Chinese construction projects, an underreported phenomenon that represents one-third of Chinese construction projects abroad.[31] In trade of physical goods, mechanical and electrical products (e.g., machinery, vehicles, and telecommunications equipment) made up nearly half (46 percent), with manufactured goods accounting for at least another quarter.[32] Textiles and chemicals likely constitute the majority of the remainder. China's African exports are also diversifying and moving up the value chain. From 2000 to 2012, exports have shifted primarily to textiles and low-end machinery. Chinese agricultural exports to Africa have increased by nearly 60 percent since 2009, reaching $2.5 billion.[33]

China's Natural Resource Imports

China imports the vast majority of its natural resources from regions other than Africa, notably the Middle East, Australia, and Latin America. However, the monetary value of African imports underrepresents their importance to China's economic security. African resources are an important element of supply diversification, lessening the risk of interrupted supply by spreading to multiple sources.[34] Oil is the largest African export to China (constituting 66 percent of all African exports to China), followed by iron ore, cotton, diamonds, timber, and copper.[35]

China has assumed a strong position in African mining sectors and imports more African minerals and metals than the United States.[36] African sources are important for several industrial inputs. Chinese sources express anxiety over resource supply security, partic-

---

[31] IOSC, 2013b.

[32] IOSC, 2013b.

[33] IOSC, 2013b. Data can be directly derived from United Nations, undated(a).

[34] See Yergin, 2006.

[35] USGS, 2013b.

[36] According to a 2012 editorial on *People's Daily Online*, because "most safe investment destinations have already been occupied by Western companies, . . . the remaining destinations are mostly full of trouble or dangers, leaving Chinese companies few choices." See *People's Daily Online*, ed., "Overseas Chinese Firms Face Security Risks," February 6, 2012a.

ularly over energy, iron, copper, bauxite, and potash; lead, zinc, and gold are also considered important.[37] Africa's reserves of oil, gas, iron, copper, and gold therefore hold obvious value.

China's growing stake in African oil and heavy state footprint have caused anxiety in the West over the potential for resource conflicts. As addressed in greater detail in this report's conclusions, such anxieties typically do not reflect how global commodity markets work in general, or African and Chinese realities in particular.

As noted above, China is a latecomer to international oil importing, having been an oil exporter until 1993. Despite becoming the world's second-largest importer of oil, its firms still lack the experience, relationships, and market penetration of the international oil firms.[38] Only in 2012 did China's oil imports from Africa (62.6 million tons) surpass those of the United States (59.7 million tons), and they remain far behind Europe's (143.8 million tons).[39] Of China's oil imports, 24 percent come from Africa, and more than half of those come from Angola.[40]

China's national oil companies (NOCs) are relative neophytes in the international oil market and have a relatively small but growing presence in Africa. In contrast to their strengths in mining and construction, Chinese firms remain secondary players in most of Africa's oil industry. Chinese NOC investment in Africa is currently around 8 percent of total international oil company investment.[41] Of the four African states that produce significant amounts of oil—Nigeria, Algeria, Angola, and Libya—Chinese firms are heavily invested only in Angola.[42] Much of Chinese oil investment is in areas where risk or

---

[37] *People's Daily Online*, ed., "China Will Run Short of 25 Kinds of Minerals by 2020," February 27, 2012b. See also The Jamestown Foundation, *China Brief*, Vol. 11, No. 15, August 12, 2011.

[38] Downs, 2009.

[39] Oil imports derived from International Energy Agency, 2012.

[40] U.S. Energy Information Administration, 2013a.

[41] Brown, 2012, p. 74.

[42] Nigeria produces 2.6 mbpd; Algeria, 2.1 mbpd; Angola, 2.0 mbpd; and Libya, 1.8 mbpd. Egypt, the next-largest producer, produces 680,000 bpd. (U.S. Energy Information Administration, 2013a.)

political limitations deter investment by Western firms.[43] This has led to a stronger Chinese position on the fringes of Africa's oil market, where firms can gain hydrocarbons, experience, and employment, but face an increased risk of disruption or investment loss. As such, Chinese firms have been large players in Angola, the Sudans, and the Republic of the Congo and are seeking to grow in other major producers, particularly Nigeria.

Contrary to popular perceptions, Chinese NOCs operate relatively independently from Beijing's political direction, reflecting profit-seeking behavior more than geopolitical behavior.[44] *State-owned* should not be assumed to be synonymous with *state-controlled*, as state-owned firms (like commercial ones) regularly avoid regulation and oversight in the pursuit of profit.[45] China's NOCs have proven difficult for Beijing to oversee (such as bidding directly against each other for assets despite Beijing's disapproval). China's NOCs have used relatively inexpensive state capital to outbid international oil companies and other state-owned NOCs for oil contracts in Africa, with a preference for ownership (equity oil) rather than production alone. Alarm over Chinese equity oil in Africa often ignores or misrepresents two fundamental realities of global oil commerce. First, as oil is traded in a globally fungible market, each barrel produced by Chinese investment adds to the global supply pool. That is, for each barrel of equity oil that China produces, it is buying one less barrel from the global oil market. As such, rather than threatening U.S. or European energy security, Chinese equity investments increase global oil supply (often from underinvested sources) and marginally lower global prices over the long term. Given transportation costs and refining characteristics, a great deal (probably the majority) of Chinese equity oil is not shipped to China,

---

43 Erica Downs, "The Fact and Fiction of Sino-African Energy Relations," *China Security*, Vol. 3, No. 3, 2007.

44 Downs, 2009.

45 See Lieberthal and Lampton, 1992; Mertha, 2009.

but is instead sold by Chinese NOCs for profit on the international market, with Europe a frequent destination.[46]

Second, Chinese firms outbidding Western firms (and often overpaying) for African oil is no strategic threat to U.S. energy security, though it can raise issues of fairness of commercial competition. The relatively large footprint of the Chinese state in China's oil finance reflects the state-owned nature of its firms (alongside state-owned firms of Norway, Japan, and India, for example) and its financial system. There is not a private-sector alternative in the Chinese case to pursue global oil deals. As several energy analysts have noted, Beijing takes a state-centric view of energy security and has a tendency to prefer ownership of assets rather than give full confidence to international markets.[47] This reflects China's socialist economy in transition, its preference for self-sufficiency, and relative inexperience as a major oil importer. However, this is quite distinct from state control or zero-sum geostrategic resource competition, for which there is no evidentiary base. In sum, the belief that China's oil activities in Africa represent a coordinated geopolitical strategy to dominate oil resources

[46] Calculating the amount of equity oil that Chinese firms sell on the international market rather than deliver to China is difficult for several reasons. In addition to issues of data availability, prices can change for a host of reasons that alter the financial incentives for determining crude contracts and ultimate destination: arbitrage between importing countries, long-haul shipping rates, and differences in grades of crude that are a better match for different refineries, to name a few. The International Energy Agency (2012) suggests that "only a portion" of Chinese equity oil returns to China. More important than the actual percentage, however, is that market incentives rather than geopolitical machinations tend to drive such decisions. As Erica Downs explains, "In terms of access to physical barrels, whether the overseas equity oil of the Chinese oil companies would be available to consumers in China during a crisis depends on the nature of the crisis, the location of the investments and whether the Chinese oil companies have title to the oil or title to the revenue. In the event of a conflict with the United States over Taiwan, a [strategic petroleum reserve] would be more helpful to China than overseas equity barrels" (Erica Downs, "The Chinese Energy Security Debate," *The China Quarterly*, Vol. 177, March 2004). For further analysis, see Julie Jiang and Jonathan Sinton, *Overseas Investments by Chinese National Oil Companies: Assessing the Drivers and Impacts*, International Energy Agency, Information Paper, February 2011, p. 17; and Dan Shalmon and Henry Lee, "Searching for Oil: China's Oil Strategies in Africa," in Robert Rotberg, ed., *China into Africa: Trade, Aid, and Influence*, Washington, D.C.: Brookings Institution, 2008.

[47] Downs, 2009.

in light of supply insecurity badly misrepresents the global, Chinese, and African oil sectors.

Sino-African Capital Flows

China has become a major source of financial capital for African economies. Estimates of the volume of these capital flows vary widely.[48] Compiling and comparing reliable data is complicated by the heavy use of tax shelters and intermediaries, private organizations that do not fully report their activities, transparency and reporting issues for both the source and recipient, and methodological and definitional differences across sources.[49] China has a history of poor statistical reporting both domestically and abroad, generated in part by China's size, complexity, and poor links between local and national governments.[50] Officially published Chinese figures on financial flows tend to be less detailed, and they identify and calculate some flows differently than their Organisation for Economic Co-operation and Development (OECD) counterparts.[51] A full exploration of these issues is beyond the scope of this report and unnecessary to understand the broad contours and strategic significance of China's capital flows to Africa. Deeply researched sources exist for those wishing to pursue these issues.[52] This report generalizes from the best available sources to estimate and

---

[48] To quote Ambassador David H. Shinn, "I have concluded that no one, including no one in China, knows the answer" to how much Chinese companies and individuals have invested in Africa (David H. Shinn, "China's Investments in Africa," China's U.S. Focus, November 1, 2012).

[49] Reputable sources have produced remarkably divergent numbers on Chinese financial flows to African states.

[50] The Heritage Foundation and American Enterprise Institute, 2012. For more on the history of Chinese statistical veracity and local-national reporting issues, see John Bryan Starr, *Understanding China: A Guide to China's Economy, History, and Political Structure*, New York: Hill and Wang, 2001. See also Shirk, 2007.

[51] See also GAO, 2013, pp. 38–39.

[52] The definitive source is Brautigam, 2009. For updated empirical data on Chinese investments and contracts, see The Heritage Foundation and American Enterprise Institute, 2012.

bound relevant Chinese flows in three major categories: FDI, loans and export credits, and foreign aid.[53]

State-owned policy banks play the dominant role in facilitating Chinese financial flows into Africa. The China Development Bank and Export-Import Bank of China play the largest roles, having also financed much of China's domestic development. China's state-centric political economy allows political leaders to dedicate investment and loans to a greater degree than in countries oriented more toward free markets.[54] Being state-owned, the banks are arguably less concerned with immediate return on investment than their Western counterparts, with a larger focus on long-term development and market access. This is not synonymous with financial flows being directed by Beijing solely toward strategic or foreign policy goals; the majority of China's financial flows into Africa are profit-seeking rather than geopolitically motivated.[55] Beijing generally eschews attaching political, human rights, or corruption-related stipulations to finance, with the exception that the recipient must honor Beijing's "One China" policy regarding Taiwan.

While most major economies leverage export credit agencies and political instruments to expand trade (the U.S. Export Import Bank, for example), the larger role of the Chinese state in its overseas economic relationships has received much attention. Given that China retains a large state sector in its domestic economy, such a larger role is unavoidable without a structural reorganization of the Chinese economy. The difference between the United States and China (as well as India, Japan, and other states featuring large state-owned sectors) in

[53] FDI is defined here as the founding of, or acquisition of a managing interest in, a commercial entity within a foreign country. Generally, FDI takes place when sufficient resource potential, human capital, or internal market potential within a foreign country makes ownership of businesses or assets therein attractive. FDI, therefore, tends to move toward more-established and stable countries. Loans, and contracted projects (such as infrastructure), incur less risk and tend to be more widely distributed.

[54] It should be noted that this active state role in investment decisions can lead to poor investment choices. See Carl E. Walter and Fraser J. T. Howie, *Red Capitalism: The Fragile Financial Foundation of China's Extraordinary Rise*, Singapore: Wiley, 2011.

[55] See Mertha, 2009.

the use of state financing to expand exports is more a matter of degree than of pure dichotomy.

Further, Chinese investment, trade, aid, and senior leadership visits are far less correlated in a unified geopolitical strategy than is commonly assumed. While the DRC and Niger are probably the second- and third-largest destinations for Chinese FDI into Africa (behind South Africa), they account for 2 percent and 0.2 percent of Sino-African trade, respectively.[56] Conversely, Angola accounts for nearly 20 percent of China's trade with Africa, yet receives less than 5 percent of Chinese FDI.[57] Chinese aid (in the form of grants and zero-interest loans) has been spread fairly evenly around Africa, with no apparent correlation to resource-rich countries.[58] With respect to senior political visits, Egypt, Tanzania, South Africa, and Morocco have seen the most-frequent visits from China's top leaders since 1995; of these, only South Africa is a major economic partner.[59] This is not to say that China's financial relations with Africa are free from politicization, and Chinese businesses can usually find more government financing and preferable rates for business ventures in Africa than their Western counterparts relying more heavily upon commercial banks. However, popular perceptions of trade and investment being subordinated to, and driven by, a coordinated geopolitical strategy by Beijing are well off the mark.[60]

While primarily commercially driven, Chinese finance currently lacks several important safeguards that regulate capital flows from OECD countries. Most importantly, loans for OECD states are scrutinized to ensure sustainability, avoiding debt-financing schemes that promise short-term development gains in exchange for long-term debts

---

[56] Sarah Baynton-Glen, *Beyond Trade—China-Africa Investment Trends*, Standard Chartered Bank, Global Research, GR12JA, February 22, 2012, p. 3.

[57] Baynton-Glen, 2012.

[58] Deborah Brautigam, "Chinese Development Aid in Africa: What, Where, Why, and How Much?" in Ligang Song and Jane Golley, eds., *Rising China: Global Challenges and Opportunities*, Canberra, Australia: Australian National University, 2011.

[59] Brautigam, 2013a.

[60] See Brautigam, 2009.

that may prove ultimately unsustainable for African governments. This is particularly dangerous in loans for infrastructure development; if the infrastructure in question is not maintained properly, it will cease functioning, while the debt accrued to build it will remain. Without such scrutiny, it remains to be seen if development projects based on more *laissez-faire* Chinese loans generate debt traps for African states, in turn creating political issues of debt forgiveness between Beijing and African capitals. This infrastructure-debt trap has occurred previously, most notably in Chinese financing of the Tanzania-Zambia railway, which fell into disrepair and required Chinese debt forgiveness.[61] Such debt burdens could fall on OECD shoulders as well, because African states may seek broad-based debt restructuring in response to national budgets thrown out of alignment, in part, by poorly designed Chinese infrastructure loans. This does not imply a deliberate strategy by either Beijing or African states but the potential second-order effect of new Chinese capital movements that lack OECD safeguards.[62]

Foreign Direct Investment

Africa is far from a leading destination for Chinese FDI but is rising rapidly, up from 1 percent of China's total outgoing FDI in 2000 to at least 3 percent in 2010. Since 2009, Chinese FDI into Africa has grown at roughly 20 percent annually. As stated in Chapter Two, this occurs as part of the wider context of Beijing's "Go Global" initiative, encouraging Chinese firms to invest globally. Official Chinese Ministry of Finance figures show more than $2.5 billion in FDI to African states in 2012, up from $392 million in 2005 but down from highs of $5.4 billion in 2008 and $3.2 billion in 2011.[63] Moreover, due in large part to the use of tax havens and to exchange controls, this figure likely understates Chinese investment into Africa considerably. The China Global Investment Tracker cites $10 billion of gross Chinese FDI proj-

---

[61] Amy Fallon, "Throwing the Tanzania-Zambia Railway a Lifeline," *Inter Press Service*, December 11, 2013.

[62] I credit Dr. Bob Sutter for pointing out this potential dynamic.

[63] Baynton-Glen, 2012, p. 3; Brautigam, 2013b. The decrease in FDI from 2008 to 2011 is likely due to the global financial crisis.

ects in Africa in 2011,[64] above U.S. investment in 2009 and 2010 (both slightly above $9 billion annually) and considerably greater than U.S. flows in 2011 ($5.1 billion).[65] More investment growth is likely; in 2012, then-President Hu Jintao promised an additional $20 billion of Chinese financing to African states.[66]

Africa's share is still dwarfed by Chinese investment in other Asian states (over half of outgoing FDI), followed by Latin America and Europe. The growth of Chinese investment has, however, been significant for African recipients. Chinese sources accounted for 16 percent of FDI to Africa in 2011, up from less than 1 percent in 2003, a twentyfold increase.[67] While annual investment is potentially approaching Western levels, cumulative Chinese investment in Africa remains behind France (around $58 billion), the United States ($57 billion), and the United Kingdom ($48 billion).[68] Official Chinese figures cite $21 billion in cumulative Chinese FDI into Africa through 2012, which appears to underestimate Chinese FDI at least by half.[69] It should be noted that China is not alone in having difficulties tracking FDI into Africa.

Historically, like the United States and European Union, China's outgoing FDI has been concentrated on natural resources. Chinese FDI has played a pivotal role in some states' extractive industries, most

---

64 The Heritage Foundation and American Enterprise Institute, 2012. Tracking only investments of more than $100 million in value estimates a $40 billion investment value alone. See also Brautigam, 2013a; GAO, 2013, pp. 38–39; and Shinn, 2011a. The data discrepancies stem from the use of third-party intermediaries (such as Hong Kong) for direct investment, a lack of detailed and publicly available data published by China on outgoing FDI, and inconsistencies in defining FDI in Chinese sources.

65 For flow data from OECD states, see Organisation for Economic Co-Operation and Development, "OECD Statistics," web tool, undated.

66 See Chinese Central Television, "Chinese President Hu Delivers Keynote Speech at China-Africa Meeting," July 19, 2012, for the speech by Chairman Hu Jintao at the Forum on China-Africa Cooperation.

67 Brown, 2012, pp. 17–20.

68 Shinn, 2011a, p 17.

69 Ministry of Commerce of the People's Republic of China, "Foreign Investment," website, various years.

notably in rebuilding Angola's ravaged infrastructure and oil industry and establishing Sudan's oil sector.[70] Cumulatively, South Africa has been the dominant recipient, but Chinese FDI flows have diversified somewhat over the past five years. The top ten recipients account for more than 70 percent of FDI, with South Africa leading at roughly 20 percent.[71] More than 90 percent of Chinese FDI likely flows through SOEs, about half of which is directed toward oil projects.[72]

Chinese Loans, Credits, and Foreign Aid

The largest source of Chinese capital flows into Africa likely consists of loans, export credits, and buyer credits, either to Chinese businesses operating in Africa or to African governments and firms themselves.[73] China's state banks offer both commercially competitive and concessional loans and export credits, with commercial the majority.[74]

China has not been a leading contributor of economic assistance (or *aid*) in a strict OECD definition.[75] China's officially reported annual aid to Africa has grown steadily from $550 million in 2000 to $2.5 billion in 2011, representing about half of China's total aid bud-

---

[70] Brown, 2012, p. 18.

[71] Bayton-Glen 2012, p. 2

[72] Gamache, Hammer, and Jones, 2013. Large holdings of FDI in Africa include the China National Offshore Oil Company, China National Petroleum Corporation, China Petroleum and Chemical Corporation (Sinopec), and China National Machinery Industry Corp (Sinomach).

[73] See The Heritage Foundation and American Enterprise Institute, 2012.

[74] See Brautigam, 2009; 2011.

[75] According to China's 2011 foreign aid white paper, aid is split roughly between grants, zero-interest loans, and concessional loans. The paper states, "By the end of 2009, China had provided a total of 256.29 billion yuan [$37.7 billion] in aid to foreign countries, including 106.2 billion yuan [$15.6 billion; 41 percent] in grants, 76.54 billion yuan [$11.3 billion; 30 percent] in interest-free loans and 73.55 billion yuan [$10.8 billion 29 percent] in concessional loans" (IOSC, *China's Foreign Aid*, White Paper, Beijing, April 2011). Broadly speaking, overseas development assistance consists of grants, zero-interest loans, or loans with an interest rate so low as to be considered concessional. See Brautigam, 2011.

get.[76] For comparison, the United States was Africa's largest donor in 2009 at $7.2 billion, followed by the World Bank ($4.1 billion) and France ($3.4 billion).[77]

Rather than aid grants, Chinese sources instead tend to offer commercially attractive loan terms and credits (lower interest rates, grace periods, and longer repayment periods) to businesses, governments, and projects in Africa.[78] What constitutes a *concessional loan* (a loan with such low interest and agreeable terms as to be considered aid) in practice is debatable,[79] particularly considering that China's abundant capital reserves and "Go Global" investment push likely incentivizes accepting higher investment risk, lower rates, and longer repayment periods than many Western sources of finance. However, Deborah Brautigam, a leading authority on Chinese aid to Africa, estimates that concessional loans could add as much as $8 billion to China's 2011 "aid" to Africa.[80]

Regardless of how aid is calculated, the majority of China's loan and credit activity in Africa is commercial in nature, with much dedi-

---

[76] Transparency issues, ambiguous definitions of *aid*, differences between promises of aid and delivery, and the packaging of aid with loans complicate precise calculation of aid. Shinn (2011a) estimates between $1.4 billion and $2.7 billion (p. 17); Brautigam (2009) suggests closer to $2.5 billion, in line with Chinese Ministry of Commerce statistics. In comparison, the World Bank ($4.1 billion), the United States ($7.2 billion), and France ($3.4 billion) give considerably more-clearly defined "foreign aid." On aid to Africa constituting half the budget, see Brautigam, 2009, p. 207. Chinese figures indicate that state aid has grown by 29.4 percent annually between 2004 and 2009, and 46.7 percent of total Chinese aid was committed to Africa in 2009. See IOSC, 2011; and Deborah Brautigam, "Chinese Aid: How Much?" *China in Africa: The Real Story*, blog post, October 14, 2013c.

[77] See Brautigam, 2011.

[78] "As in the case of investment, it is exceedingly difficult to measure China's aid. China does not publish country-by-country aid disbursement figures, which are treated as a state secret. In the Chinese context, it is difficult to determine what constitutes aid as most of its big programs are concessionary loans. The concessionary aspect of the loan is legitimate aid, but the principal must be paid back unless China eventually cancels the debt, which it has a record of doing for the poorest African countries" (Shinn, 2012).

[79] For example, OECD and Export-Import Bank of China definitions for *concessional loan* vary.

[80] Brautigam, 2013c.

cated toward matching China's strength in construction or desire for resource projects with African states' need for affordable development and infrastructure.[81] Many infrastructure and natural resource financing offers provide competitive rates in exchange for commercially attractive aspects for Chinese firms—for example, dedicating funds to a resource project, with the loan guaranteed and China repaid by a share of the resource production (*resource-backed loans*); contracting Chinese firms for all or part of the project; and sourcing materials and labor from Chinese firms.[82]

It should be pointed out that using resource-backed loans, and sometimes associated equity and corruption issues, predates Chinese finance on the continent. As demonstrated in Angola (arguably the most prominent case of problematic Chinese resource-backed loans), Western banks initiated resource-backed loans and were deeply involved in the ethical conundrums surrounding Angola's 40 years of conflict.[83] China was actually on the receiving end of the first oil-for-infrastructure-projects model, initiated by Japanese banks in the 1990s.[84] There is nothing inherently nefarious about resource-backed loans; through this arrangement, developing resource exporters are able to leverage

---

[81] Between 20 and 25 percent of China's construction projects in Africa are financed by Chinese banks or the Chinese government, constituting around $10 billion.

[82] See Brautigam, 2009.

[83] See Brautigam, 2009. The Angola case is instructive for the distance between media representation of foreign finance to African states and its realities. As is often cited, China's offer of "no-strings-attached" finance came at a time when the IMF was close to negotiating Luanda into a deal meant to address Angola's persistent corruption problems. Less widely reported, however, is that Angola had failed in at least four IMF programs in the previous decade and that Germany and France also broke ranks with the IMF to gain access. Further, after the Chinese loan, a large group of Western banks arranged larger oil-backed loans, and the U.S. Export-Import Bank provided nearly $1 billion to Angola to purchase Boeing aircraft. Both China and African states are likely puzzled at the attention given the smaller, yet generally similar, Chinese loans. It should also be noted that while China's financial offer was more generous, it was not a giveaway; it reduced interest by 1 percent from the standard rate, allowing a five-year initial grace period, and lengthened the loan term from four years to 12. Cases such as this suggest that both Chinese and U.S. visions of the other's involvement in Africa, reflecting bilateral strategic distrust, are prone to confirmation bias, comparing a partial representation of the other's involvement with an idealized vision of their own.

[84] See Brautigam, 2009, pp. 273–277.

what they have in abundance (resources) to obtain what they often lack (infrastructure to develop the resources and acceptable loan terms). In exchange for accepting higher risk, longer repayment, and lower interest, Chinese (or other) firms obtain resources and construction projects.[85] Nor are all such loans associated with oil, or with infrastructure development. Ghana has conducted resource-backed loans based on cocoa beans, and despite the widespread application of the oil-for-infrastructure label to resource-backed loans in general, that practice is largely limited to Angola and the Republic of the Congo.[86] Chinese banks have extended resource-backed loans to at least seven African states, totaling more than $14 billion.[87] Chinese SOEs have been the dominant recipient of Chinese export credits for business in Africa, but Beijing has announced a $1 billion fund to support private firms.[88]

Special Economic Zones

In support of Beijing's wider "Go Global" commercial strategy, the CCP's eleventh Five-Year Plan in 2006 called for a global expansion of Chinese *special economic zones* (SEZs).[89] China has initiated six SEZs within Africa: Egypt, Ethiopia, Mauritius, Zambia, and two in Nigeria (Ogun and Lekki).[90] The purpose of SEZs is to attract Chinese and other foreign investment and to reduce the costs, risks, and delays of doing business in Africa. SEZs function by incentivizing firms—through subsidies, tax breaks (both Chinese and host nation), and cheap loans—to move or establish businesses within the zone. The zones also generally have expedited bureaucratic processes and less red tape. The SEZs are intended to increase Chinese exports and demonstrate Chinese investment in Africa. In addition, SEZs can assist

---

[85] See IOSC, 2010; 2013b.

[86] Deborah Brautigam, "China's Foreign Aid: The Economist Still Doesn't Get It," *China in Africa: The Real Story*, blog post, January 22, 2012.

[87] Brautigam, 2010a.

[88] Brown, 2012, p. 66.

[89] China Internet Information Center, undated.

[90] Deborah Brautigam and Tang Xiaoyang, "African Shenzhen: China's Special Economic Zones in Africa," *Journal of Modern African Studies*, Vol. 49, No. 1, 2011.

China's economic rebalancing, potentially allowing lower-skilled and more–environmentally hazardous sectors to be moved offshore as Chinese industries move up the value chain. SEZs represent Chinese investment in the African industrial base, which is sorely lacking (roughly 1 percent of aggregate GDP).[91] SEZs historically take years (if not decades) to generate significant operations, and China's African zones appear to be no exception. Much of their eventual benefit to African states, and to Beijing, will depend on whether they function as meaningful areas for technology and skills transfer to African states, or as Chinese enclaves.

Chinese Arms Exports to Africa

The character of China's arms exports to Africa has changed markedly since the Maoist period. Beginning with government-sponsored gifting of weapons to African governments aligned with it during the Cold War, China's arms industry transitioned to a more commercial footing during the early post-Mao period. Initially, Chinese firms competed on whole-system exports (rather than small arms or component parts), with exports reaching a high point in the mid- to late 1980s.[92] Within Africa, Egypt in particular was a major destination for Chinese military hardware, including 80 F-7 fighter jets, six *Romeo*-class submarines, three frigates, and 13 fast-attack craft.[93] However, the poor performance of Chinese systems during several conflicts in the 1980s and early 1990s hurt the export sector, and Chinese firms lost their market share primarily to Russian and Eastern European industries.[94] Muscled out of the profitable higher-technology markets, China's state-owned arms manufacturers likely continue to operate at large losses and with

---

91 Brown, 2012, p. 62.

92 In 1990, Chinese exports made up 8 percent of the global arms market (Ian Taylor, "China's Arms Transfers to Africa and Political Violence," *Terrorism and Political Violence*, Vol. 25, 2013, p. 458).

93 Shinn and Eisenman, 2012, p. 167.

94 The most notable conflicts are the Iran-Iraq War and First Gulf War. See Taylor, 2013, p. 458.

large debts.[95] The effect of these losses became more acute when the CCP divested the PLA of its holdings in China's arms industry in 1998, over CCP concerns about the PLA's role in China's economy and the diversion of military attention toward business concerns.[96] Despite these setbacks, Chinese industry has been successful in small-arms trade and low-price manufacturing. This has facilitated a large role in the African arms sector that has spanned several decades. The losses and debts of China's arms companies underscore their willingness to be aggressive in conducting business despite political sensitivities.

China is likely the largest single supplier of small arms and light weapons to Africa, with exports accounting for more than 25 percent of the total African arms market in 2011, and 17 percent of China's total arms exports that year.[97] According to the Stockholm International Peace Research Institute, China provided more than $2.5 billion in arms to Africa from 2002 to 2010, selling to at least 16 African states.[98] Nigeria was the largest recipient, taking 35 percent of Chinese exports to Africa. The scale of arms transfers is noteworthy, because arms sales are significant predictors of increased political violence in Africa.[99] Furthermore, there is a widely noted lack of transparency from Beijing over the volume of sales, role of the central government therein, China's export policies, and its enforcement of them. The lack

---

95 See Evan S. Medeiros, *Analyzing China's Defense Industries and the Implications for Chinese Military Modernization*, Santa Monica, Calif.: RAND Corporation, CT-217, 2004.

96 The CCP felt that the PLA's business empire distracted it from its principal national security duties, provided it with an independent power base, and did not align with broader liberalization of the Chinese economy. See Mulvenon, 2001.

97 Figures derived from Stockholm International Peace Research Institute, "Arms Transfers Database," web tool, undated. This figure does not include South Africa. From 2002 to 2009, Chinese firms transferred $1.4 billion in conventional arms to North Africa and $1.1 billion to sub-Saharan Africa. These consisted of 590 armored personnel carriers and light vehicles, 390 artillery pieces, 220 aircraft, 130 anti-ship missiles, 56 minor naval surface combatants, and 20 tanks and self-propelled guns. See Richard F. Grimmett, "Conventional Arms Transfers to Developing Nations, 2002–2009," Washington, D.C.: Congressional Research Service, CRS Report for Congress, September 10, 2010, pp. 52–58.

98 Grimmett, 2010.

99 Cassidy Craft and Joseph P. Smaldone, "The Arms Trade and the Incidence of Political Violence in Sub-Saharan Africa, 1967–97," *Journal of Peace Research*, Vol. 39, No. 6, 2002.

of transparency has made the data on African arms trade questionable; for example, it has caused several Chinese firms to be excluded from the Stockholm International Peace Research Institute's arms-transfer data, thereby almost certainly underrepresenting Chinese arms sales.[100] Beijing has also reportedly not submitted arms exports data to the U.N. Register on Conventional Arms since 1996, ostensibly due to anger over U.S. arms sales to Taiwan being included.[101]

It is unsurprising, therefore, that arms sales are an area where Beijing's desire to keep political and commercial affairs distinct has proven problematic for China's international reputation. China's relatively apolitical approach to arms sales in Africa has created friction with the United States and other members of the international community.[102] Chinese firms have sold weapons to states engaged in civil conflict, as well as pariah states with security services engaged in human rights abuses. China is certainly not alone in this respect; Russia, Ukraine, Belarus, Moldova, and Singapore have strong weapons trade in Africa, and many states' weapons are used in African conflicts. Small weapons transfers within Africa are common and facilitated by poor border controls, robust black markets, and smuggling networks.

With regard to pariah states, several examples stand out. Chinese arms companies have reportedly sold jet fighters, vehicles, radars, and radio jamming equipment to Zimbabwe.[103] There have been reports of Chinese firms accepting ivory as payment from Harare.[104] Chinese arms firms have been accused of selling arms to both sides of African

[100] Taylor, 2013, p. 460.

[101] Taylor, 2013, p. 461. For the Taiwan issue, see United Nations, *Disarmament Yearbook 2006*, Vol. 31, New York: Office for Disarmament Affairs, 2007.

[102] *Apolitical* refers here to Beijing's comparative lack of political reservations about conducting arms sales with pariah states, those involved in civil conflict, or those accused of human rights violations. See Amnesty International, *People's Republic of China: Sustaining Conflict and Human Rights Abuses: The Flow of Arms Accelerates*, New York: Amnesty International, 2006.

[103] The sources for the examples in this paragraph stem primarily from Taylor, 2013, pp. 460–472; and Shinn and Eisenman, 2012.

[104] Taylor, 2013, p. 466; Lukas Jeuck, *Arms Transfers to Zimbabwe: Implications for an Arms Treaty*, Stockholm International Peace Research Institute, Background Paper, March 2011.

conflicts, including the Ethiopian-Eritrean war of the late 1990s.[105] During the Darfur conflict and Sudanese civil war, Chinese firms supplied 12 F-7 fighter jets, tanks, and artillery to Khartoum, and assisted in building Sudanese weapon factories.[106] Finally, Western nongovernmental organizations reported Sudanese troops working alongside Chinese oil firms to seize oil-producing areas and protect production.[107] As Ian Taylor points out, arms exports to Sudan and Zimbabwe are inherently politically sensitive and almost certainly could not have taken place without at least tacit backing from Beijing.[108] In 2011, Chinese state-run arms companies reportedly offered roughly $200 million of military hardware to Muammar Gaddafi's regime during the final weeks of the conflict, despite U.N. resolutions banning such activity and Beijing having made overtures to the rebels' National Transitional Council.[109] China's Foreign Ministry claimed that the firms involved did not inform Beijing of their attempted sales and that no weapons were shipped. Other troubling arms sales have been reported, including to Sierra Leone, the DRC, and the Great Lakes region. In 1995, shortly after the worst episodes of Hutu-Tutsi violence, Human Rights Watch claims to have discovered 13 covert shipments of weapons (three of which violated international arms embargoes) from Chinese firms to Burundi via Dar-es-Salaam, with cargo destination and content mislabeled.[110]

See also AsiaNews, "Weapons for Ivory: The Illegal Trade Between Bejiing and Zimbabwe," November 17, 2004.

[105] Shinn and Eisenman, 2012, p. 7.

[106] Taylor, 2013, pp. 460–472; Shinn and Eisenman, 2012, p. 7.

[107] Medecins Sans Frontieres, *Violence, Health, and Access to Aid in Unity State/Western Upper Nile, Sudan*, Holland, April 2002, p. 16. See also Refugees International, *Sudan: Oil Exploration Fueling Displacement in the South*, Bulletin, June 14, 2006.

[108] Taylor, 2013, pp. 460–472.

[109] Shinn and Eisenman, 2012, p. 240. See also CNN Wire, "China Denies Report, Says It Did Not Sell Weapons to Libya," September 6, 2011; and Michael Wines and Betsy Apple, "Beijing Says Qaddafi Officials Sought Chinese Arms Supplies," *The New York Times*, September 5, 2011.

[110] Human Rights Watch, *Stoking the Fires: Military Assistance and Arms Trafficking in Burundi*, New York: Human Rights Watch Arms Project, December 1997.

Sino-African Political Relations

The nature and character of China's national, provincial, and local government relationships with African counterparts vary widely. This section will focus on the national-level phenomena: bilateral and multilateral relations, diplomatic engagement, soft-power initiatives, and media outreach.

China's Diplomatic Engagement and Political Relations

China has been busier than the United States over the past ten years in political engagement with African states. In terms of senior visits, China has sent three times as many heads of state as the Bush and Obama administrations during that span, and Beijing has hosted African heads of state much more frequently than Washington has.[111] Chinese President Xi Jinping's first overseas trip, in March 2013, was to Russia, Tanzania, South Africa, and the Republic of the Congo. In the 1990s and 2000s, the Chinese foreign minister's first overseas visit in every year was to an African country.[112] In addition, there has been heavy mid-level government-to-government engagement.[113] Interestingly, high-level bilateral engagements do not correlate strongly with China's economic interests in Africa.

It should be noted that neither Beijing nor Washington simply dictates terms to African political and commercial leaders. On the contrary, as seen frequently during the Cold War, African leaders often bargain hard and promote their own interests.[114]

African heads of state tend to make sunnier statements toward China than they do toward the United States, and opinion polls in

---

[111] Brown, 2012, p. 36. China's previous President Hu visited 18 African countries in four visits during his presidency. See Xinhua, "China to Announce New Measures on Cooperation with Africa: Vice FM," *China Radio International English*, July 12, 2012b.

[112] Shinn, 2011a, p. 18.

[113] Brown, 2012, p. 36.

[114] I credit Michael Shurkin for this point. See also Shinn and Eisenman, 2012.

Africa show generally positive views of China on the continent.[115] At the government level, criticism of China is often short-lived and does not result in enduring policy changes. Sino-African economic ties tend to run independent of political currents; changes to Beijing-friendly African governments have not meaningfully affected business ties in Ghana, Guinea, Niger, and Zambia.[116] Opposition leaders, even those critical of China during their campaigns (such as Zambia's Michael Sata[117]) tend to warm to China once in office. Similarly, contrary to frequent media assertions, China does not reflexively side with authoritarian governments in Africa. It is instead pragmatic; for example, consider the diversity in China's interactions with democratic (Botswana, Mauritius), authoritarian (Zimbabwe), and Islamist (Sudan) states. Beijing has also, when allowed by the host nation, engaged opposition parties within a coalition government (hosting Zimbabwe's Morgan Tsangarai, for example).[118]

While China's relations with African states are for the most part bilateral, the triennial Forum on China-Africa Cooperation (FOCAC) is the centerpiece of Chinese multilateral engagement with African states. Initiated in October 2000, the FOCAC brings together Chinese and African heads of state and ministry-level leaders to centralize, coordinate, and communicate China's major political and economic activities in Africa.[119] Within the FOCAC, which rotates between Beijing and African capitals, Chinese leaders announce economic and technical cooperation commitments while spending two days interact-

---

[115] Pew Global Attitudes Project, "Global Unease with Major World Powers: 47-Nation Pew Global Attitudes Survey," Pew Research Center, Public Opinion Survey, June 27, 2007, pp. 39–41; Aleksandra Gadzala and Marek Hanusch, *African Perspectives on China-Africa: Gauging Popular Perceptions and Their Economic and Political Determinants*, Afrobarometer Working Paper No. 117, January 2010, p. 18. On African leadership statements, see Shinn, 2011a, p. 18.

[116] Brautigam, 2013a.

[117] Joan Chirwa-Ngoma, "Sata Praises Chinese," *The Post (Zambia)*, April 7, 2013.

[118] Ministry of Foreign Affairs of the People's Republic of China, "Vice Premier Wang Yang Meets with Zimbabwean Prime Minister Morgan Tsvangirai," Beijing, May 23, 2013.

[119] Ministry of Foreign Affairs of the People's Republic of China, "Forum on China-Africa Cooperation," web page, undated.

ing with African heads of state. Through the FOCAC, and China's three white papers on African relations, Beijing attempts to contrast itself with the West by framing relations in terms of "mutual respect," "win-win" outcomes, and "noninterference" in domestic affairs.[120]

Soft-Power Initiatives, Media Outreach, and African Perceptions

China has also pursued multiple soft-power and prestige projects in Africa. Most notably, in January 2012 the African Union inaugurated a new headquarters complex in Addis Ababa, a $200 million facility donated by Beijing and jointly constructed.[121] China has pursued other "prestige gifts" as well, including government buildings, stadiums, and infrastructure.[122] In addition, Beijing has funded an array of engagement programs, from young leadership exchanges, Peace Corps–style foreign assistance programs, a steady presence of Chinese doctors, 29 cultural outreach centers ("Confucian Institutes") in 22 states, and radio and television broadcasting.[123] It is difficult to quantify the influence and goodwill gained by such measures, most of which are relatively nascent, and cultural gaps still appear to be obstacles to deeper Sino-African interactions.[124] However, African leaders frequently laud Chinese efforts, and these mechanisms have increased the exposure of emerging African leaders to China.

China now has a major media presence in Africa, undertaking in the past three years what the editor of Kenya's most popular newspa-

---

[120] Brown, 2012, pp. 34–38; People's Republic of China, 2006; IOSC, *China-Africa Economic and Trade Cooperation 2010*, White Paper, Beijing, December 23, 2010a; IOSC, 2013b.

[121] BBC, "African Union Opens Chinese-Funded HQ in Ethiopia," January 28, 2012a.

[122] For example, see Frank Kandu, "China to Build New Malawi Stadium," *BBC Sport*, October 31, 2012.

[123] Brown, 2012, pp. 40–43. This is not meaningfully different than the United Kingdom's British Council, French Alliance Française, or German Goethe Institute. China has offered 5,000 scholarships annually to African students for study in China. Since 1963, China has deployed more than 18,000 medical personnel for service in 46 states (Shinn, 2013).

[124] See the excellent documentary film *When China Met Africa*, dir. Marc Francis and Nick Francis, Speakit Films, October 2011.

per has called a "full-on charm offensive."[125] Beijing's interest in media expansion is likely driven by three desires: to reach out to African audiences, to respond to the growing Chinese population in Africa, and to counter a perceived neocolonial and anti-Chinese bias in Western news agencies' reporting on Africa.[126] While the CCP's official and state-run Xinhua news agency has reported from Africa for decades, China's media presence in Africa has increased markedly since 2009. In January of that year, Beijing announced a planned commitment of $6.6 billion to expand Chinese state media on the continent.[127] In early 2011, Xinhua debuted its CNC World television station, with state-run Chinese Central Television following with CCTV Africa in early 2012.[128] In December 2012, China's largest state-run English-language newspaper, *China Daily*, introduced its *Africa Weekly* newspaper.[129] Xinhua has also partnered with the Kenyan telecommunications firm Safaricom to launch sub-Saharan Africa's first mobile news service.[130] With widely distributed reporting from Xinhua (more than 20 bureaus in African states) and a mix of Chinese- and English-language programming—featuring news and human-interest media across print, radio, and television—Chinese media is expanding in Africa while many Western media outlets are reducing their presence.[131] There have been some complaints from African audiences that Chinese media have a

---

125 Andrew Jacobs, "Pursuing Soft Power, China Puts Stamp on Africa's News," *New York Times*, August 16, 2012.

126 Hu Yihan, "China Has No Colonial Designs on Africa," *China Daily*, December 9, 2011.

127 Joost Akkermans, "China Plans 45 Billion Yuan Media Expansion, Morning Post Says," *Bloomberg*, January 12, 2009.

128 For examples of CCTV Africa's television programming, see its YouTube channel.

129 David McKenzie, "Chinese Media Making Inroads into Africa," CNN, September 25, 2012.

130 Mark Kapchanga, "Changing Channels: The Rise of Chinese Media in Africa," *Think Africa Press*, February 17, 2013.

131 See, for example, BBC, "BBC World Service to Lose 73 Jobs," October 18, 2012c; and Lucinda Fleeson, "Bureau of Missing Bureaus," *American Journalism Review*, October/November 2003.

bias toward positive news and progovernment reporting, including coverage supporting the Qaddafi regime during the Libyan revolution.[132]

Despite these efforts and the comparative success of government-to-government ties, China appears in most areas to have been less successful at engaging the African public or civil society actors. Western media coverage of African pushback toward Chinese influence, however, tends to distort the causes and overstate the scale of popular African discontent.[133] Western sources tend to cite Chinese workers displacing African jobs and the supposed low quality of Chinese goods and infrastructure as sources of African resentment. However, a closer look suggests that Africans generally accept that Chinese goods are cheaper and less durable.[134] Similarly, while some infrastructure projects have been low quality, Chinese firms get a great deal of repeat business; 23 of the top 100 construction firms by revenue in Africa are Chinese.[135] While some construction projects import Chinese labor, many hire local Africans.[136]

Several issues do generate friction with local African communities, particularly in larger African states: labor and safety standards, counterfeit goods (especially medicine), environmental standards, and corporate social responsibility. It should be noted that Chinese firms struggle with these issues within China, and both Western and African firms struggle with some of them within Africa as well. These dynamics vary greatly from state to state and sector to sector. In some African states, the transfer of jobs to Africans from Chinese enterprises has not

---

[132] David Bandurski, "How China Reports the Arab World," *China Media Project: University of Hong Kong*, April 18, 2011; Colin Shek, "Chinese Media Expands Africa Presence," Al Jazeera, January 24, 2013.

[133] Barry Sautman and Yan Hairong, "African Perspectives on China-Africa Links," *China Quarterly*, Vol. 199, September 2009.

[134] See Deborah Brautigam, "African Traders in China and Substandard Goods," *China in Africa: The Real Story*, blog post, October 21, 2010b; and Tendai Musakwa, "Deborah Brautigam Discusses the U.S. and China's Relations with Africa," The China Africa Project, April 8, 2013.

[135] *Engineering News-Record*, "The Top 250 International Contractors," web page, 2013.

[136] Deborah Brautigam, "Chinese Workers Data: Anecdotes and Data," *China in Africa: The Real Story*, web page, undated; Brautigam, 2013a.

occurred as quickly as desired, because Chinese firms have brought their own staff. While this is in part due to Chinese firms responding to the terms of Chinese financing, a preference for Chinese speakers, and perhaps a bias for Chinese workers, research suggests that Chinese workers in Africa are more productive than their African counterparts. Chinese textile workers in Mozambique, for example, appear to be nearly twice as productive per day as domestic labor.[137] In addition, by undercutting the prices of local products, Chinese merchants have displaced Africans in some domestic industries and local marketplaces (most notably textiles in Mozambique), causing localized grievances.[138]

Chinese Security Behavior in Africa

The PLA plays a small role in China's African relations relative to both the United States and European Union militaries. The PLA also plays a small role relative to China's economic and political actors in Africa and to China's emerging security interests on the continent. Several security interests are emerging for China in Africa: protecting its citizens and assets, gaining experience for the PLA, and performing the security duties incumbent upon an emerging power. These interests generate at least five potential expeditionary missions for the PLA: peacekeeping, humanitarian aid and disaster relief, sea lane security, noncombatant evacuation operations (NEOs), and personnel and asset protection.[139] The PLA has started to develop some capability to execute the first four, but protecting (or freeing) Chinese citizens is chiefly left to the Ministry of Foreign Affairs and private Chinese security firms. An expanded set of future roles is conceivable. While China does not have the commitments or power projection capability at present, a future PLA may wish to project power and conduct counterterrorism operations, conventional deterrence, and more-extensive secu-

---

[137] David Haroz, "China in Africa: Symbiosis or Exploitation," *Fletcher Forum of World Affairs*, Vol. 35, No. 2, 2011.

[138] Gadzala and Hanusch, 2010, p. 6.

[139] I credit my RAND colleagues Jeff Engstrom and Cortez Cooper for this list of missions.

rity cooperation with African militaries. However, while the PLA and Ministry of Defense have increased their diplomatic outreach to African militaries, the PLA remains a regional military.

This section outlines the PLA's activities in U.N. peacekeeping operations, China's military relations in Africa, and its current efforts to protect Chinese citizens and assets therein. The section also highlights three recent and significant events in PLA history involving Africa: the 2008 Gulf of Aden counterpiracy deployment, the 2011 NEO from Libya, and the 2013 deployments to Mali and South Sudan. These events represent notable firsts for the PLA Navy, Air Force, and Army, suggesting future growth in PLA roles and capabilities.

United Nations Peacekeeping Operations

The largest area of Chinese military engagement with Africa has been the PLA's commitment to U.N. peacekeeping operations. After a long period of eschewing and criticizing such participation as foreign interference, over the past 15 years, Beijing has likely viewed U.N. participation as a means of adding to China's image as a global leader. Further, such deployments help gain operational experience for a PLA that has not seen ground combat since the 1979 incursion into Vietnam (which had decidedly mixed operational results) or major combat operations since the Korean War.[140] Since 2001, the PLA has sent approximately 11,000 military personnel to participate in 18 U.N. peacekeeping operations. China is the twelfth-largest contributor to peacekeeping operations and the leading contributor among permanent members of the Security Council.[141] It is also the sixth-largest contributor to the United Nations' peacekeeping budget, contributing just under 7 percent of the total.[142] However, this is well below the U.S. contribution (the largest

---

[140] David Michael Finkelstein, Michael A. McDevitt, and Mark A. Ryan, eds., *Chinese Warfighting: The PLA Experience Since 1949*, Armonk, N.Y.: M. E. Sharpe, Inc., 2003.

[141] IOSC, 2013a; United Nations Peacekeeping, "Troop and Police Contributors," web tool, undated.

[142] United Nations, "Financing Peacekeeping. United Nations Peacekeeping," web page, undated(b).

contributor at more than 28 percent), and smaller than the British and French contributions as well.

Until the 2012 deployments to South Sudan and Mali (see the following subsection), the PLA contingents consisted of only noncombat troops: staff officers, military observers, engineers, medical staff, and logistics support. Since 2004, China has also contributed civilian *formed police units* to U.N. missions from its domestic police forces (typically from its provincial-level border police units), distinct from PLA military police or the central government's paramilitary People's Armed Police.[143]

The PLA participates in seven of the eight current U.N. missions in Africa, involving approximately 1,500 personnel on six- to 12-month rotations. These rotations constitute nearly 75 percent of the PLA's total of U.N. peacekeeping forces.[144] These troops participate in a range of highly visible roles, including helping with electoral and judicial reforms, training police, and rehabilitating former combatants.[145] The PLA's largest overseas commitment is to the U.N. contingents in Sudan, numbering approximately 750. The PLA's peacekeeping role in Sudan is shaped by Beijing's diplomatic ties to Sudan and interest in Sudanese stability. Facing international pressure over ties to Khartoum, Beijing committed peacekeeping forces largely to demonstrate a constructive role and contain international pressure on a major oil supplier. Similarly, PLA participation in the U.N. Mission to South Sudan (UNMISS) demonstrates a constructive role for Beijing while stabilizing an area that supplies petroleum and contains significant Chinese investment.

---

[143] Craig Murray, *China to Deploy "Security Force" to UN Peacekeeping Operation in Mali*, Washington, D.C.: U.S.-China Economic and Security Review Commission, Staff Research Backgrounder, July 9, 2013, p. 2.

[144] The PLA has sent personnel to U.N. missions in the following states: Darfur, DRC, Liberia, and South Sudan, and small contingents to Cote D'Ivoire and Western Sahara. In June 2013, the PRC agreed to send around 400 PLA peacekeepers to Mali as part of a U.N. mission. The PLA is not involved in the U.N. mission to Abyei. See IOSC, 2013a; United Nations Peacekeeping, undated.

[145] Richard Weitz, "China and Africa Peacekeeping," Second Line of Defense, March 2013.

Bilateral Military Relations and Military Diplomacy

Beyond U.N. peacekeeping operations, China maintains modest but growing relations with African militaries. The PLA has bilateral relations with the 51 African states that recognize Beijing rather than Taipei, although many of these relations are not substantial. The PLA operates 16 defense attaché offices covering 30 African states, with the majority of PLA officers likely career Army intelligence officers.[146] There are 28 African states with attachés in Beijing, up from 18 in 2007.[147] The PLA sent 12 senior delegations to Africa from 2009 to 2012 and hosted 13 such delegations from African militaries.[148] The PLA's visits are not correlated with China's economic interests, although they do feature a high number of coastal states, potentially pointing to interest in replenishment locations.[149] In line with its policy of no foreign bases, China has no bases or operating locations in Africa and has publicly committed to not developing them. To date, the PLA has undertaken no major joint military exercises with an African state, although it has expressed a desire for deeper collaboration with African militaries. For example, the PLA has recently sought limited exercises and arms contracts with the Nigerian Navy to counter piracy in the Gulf of Guinea.[150] The PLA has conducted regular defense consultations only with South Africa, beginning in 2003.[151] Such consultations are likely to expand; China's

---

[146] On attaché offices, see Susan Puska, "Military Backs China's African Adventure," *Asia Times*, June 8, 2007. On intelligence officers, see Kenneth W. Allen and Eric A. McVadon, *China's Foreign Military Relations*, Washington, D.C.: Henry L. Stimson Center, 1999, p. 19.

[147] Shinn and Eisenman, 2012, p. 169.

[148] China sent delegations to Angola, Cameroon, Ethiopia, Mozambique, Namibia, Seychelles, South Africa, Tanzania (twice), Uganda, and Zambia (twice). China received delegations from Algeria, Djibouti (twice), Egypt, Equatorial Guinea, Ghana, Malawi, Mozambique, Namibia, Nigeria, Rwanda, Sierra Leone, South Africa. These lists were generated by RAND calculations of Open Source Center reporting, August 2013.

[149] I credit my RAND colleagues Larry Hanauer and Lyle Morris for this insight.

[150] Andrew Erickson and Austin Strange, "Piracy's Next Frontier: A Role for China in Gulf of Guinea Security?" *The National Interest*, December 10, 2013c.

[151] Shinn and Eisenman, 2012, pp. 169.

2010 Defense White Paper states, "China has also established mechanisms for defense (cooperation) commission meetings with Egypt."[152]

Since its 2006 Africa White Paper, China does promote training and assistance programs with officers from African militaries.[153] While the programs are still modest in scope, in August 2012, the PLA conducted its most significant training exercises with an African military to date, collaborating with the Nigerian Navy to train for security threats in the Gulf of Guinea.[154] Other programs include China donating vehicles and training equipment; sending trainers, maintenance teams, and PLA officers as liaisons; and regularly hosting African officers at China's National Defense University. Every African army has at least one colonel or brigadier general who graduated from this university.[155] However, sources suggest that the quality, curriculum, and separation of PLA and African officers detract from the value of the university's programs, and the personnel with the highest promotion potential are still sent to Western academies.[156]

China has initiated or participated in several other bilateral or multilateral military efforts involving Africa. The PLAN has sent its hospital ship, the Peace Ark, on two goodwill cruises, including a 2010 goodwill cruise visiting Djibouti, Kenya, the Seychelles, and Tanzania, among other developing states.[157] The PLA has also deployed its China International Search and Rescue team, which provides medical and rescue operations, to several states globally, including recently to Algeria.[158]

---

[152] IOSC, 2010b.

[153] People's Republic of China, 2006.

[154] Oghogho Obayuwana, "China Wants to Partner Nigeria on Gulf of Guinea," *The Guardian* (Nigeria), August 2, 2012.

[155] Horta Loro, "Defense and Military Education: A Dimension of Chinese Power," *Power and Interest News Report*, September 29, 2006.

[156] Loro, 2006.

[157] Xinhua, "International Disaster Relief Operations Obligation of China's Armed Forces," China.org, March 31, 2011.

[158] Haizhou, 2012.

The PLA Navy's Historic Deployment to the Gulf of Aden

Most significantly, since December 2008, the PLAN has participated in international efforts to protect commercial shipping from piracy in the Gulf of Aden. The ongoing deployment is the first time that Chinese warships have conducted military operations beyond the Asia Pacific since the fifteenth-century expeditions of Zheng He during the Ming Dynasty.[159] Like the navies of India, Iran, Japan, and Russia, the PLAN has operated independently from the multinational naval task forces operating in the Gulf of Aden.[160] The PLAN has escorted more than 5,000 merchant ships, about half of which were flagged in China, Taiwan, or Hong Kong, and rescued two pirated merchant vessels.[161] However, the PLAN has gradually increased its interaction with multinational partners, conducting two small counterpiracy exercises with the U.S. 5th Fleet since 2012.[162]

In addition to its counterpiracy and naval diplomacy benefits, the PLAN's patrol in the Gulf of Aden has proven valuable as modern China's first far-seas naval presence. This has provided valuable and rare firsthand experience in the realities of distant operations. In addition to the operational experience, the deployment has further helped the PLAN gain an understanding of the logistical challenges of extended operations and the resulting need for standing relationships with shore-based suppliers. The patrol has also facilitated increased port call activity in the Mediterranean, including Israel and Turkey in 2012,[163] and has increased PLAN familiarity with foreign navies.

The forward naval presence has given Beijing a supporting military option to face unexpected contingencies, something it is unlikely

---

159 Andrew Erickson and Austin Strange, *No Substitute for Experience: Chinese Antipiracy Operations in the Gulf of Aden*, Newport, R.I.: China Maritime Studies Institute, U.S. Naval War College, No. 10, October 2013a.

160 Andrew Erickson and Austin Strange, "China and the International Antipiracy Effort," *The Diplomat*, November 1, 2013b.

161 IOSC, 2013a.

162 Donna Miles, "U.S., Chinese Navies Exercise Counterpiracy in Gulf of Aden," American Forces Press Service, August 26, 2013.

163 Erickson and Strange, 2013a.

that Beijing intended when it first began the rotation in 2008. As covered in greater detail later in the subsection on the Libya evacuation, an advanced frigate from the task force was able to lend naval support the China's largest NEO to date. Similarly, in December 2013, Beijing announced that elements of the PLAN counterpiracy task force would assist in escorting Syrian chemical weapons to the U.S.-led coalition for ultimate destruction.[164] Neither operation would have been feasible in a timely manner without the forward presence granted by the Gulf of Aden patrol, given that the Chinese mainland is more than two weeks' transit to the Suez Canal (about 6,500 nautical miles).[165] It remains to be seen how the deployment will evolve, given the dramatic decline in Gulf of Aden piracy since 2011, punctuated by the lack of any successful hijackings in nine attempts during 2013.[166] The PLAN's Deputy Commander stated that a counterpiracy naval presence will remain in the Gulf of Aden through November 2014; it is uncertain if the U.N. mandate for regional counterpiracy will extend further.[167] Previous media reporting of China wanting to take the leading role in the multilateral Shared Awareness and Deconfliction mechanism, a working group to help coordinate multinational counterpiracy efforts, was likely erroneous.[168]

Despite much attention on the potential for a chain of PLAN naval bases or operating locations spanning the Indian Ocean (the "string of pearls" discourse),[169] China's replenishment locations for Indian Ocean transits have been characterized by limited resupply

164 Zhou Wa, "Warships to Help Dispose of Syrian Chemical Weapons," *China Daily USA*, December 26, 2013.

165 Andrew Erickson and Austin Strange, "China and the Far Seas," *The Diplomat*, January 10, 2014.

166 U.S. Office of Naval Intelligence, *Horn of Africa and Gulf of Guinea: Piracy Analysis and Warning Weekly (PAWW) Report*, Maritime OPINTEL Report, December 19, 2013.

167 Erickson and Strange, 2014.

168 Greg Torode, "PLA Delays Taking Lead on Piracy," *South China Morning Post*, June 21, 2010; Erickson and Strange, 2013b.

169 Daniel Kostecka, "Places and Bases: The Chinese Navy's Emerging Support Network in the Indian Ocean," *Naval War College Review*, Vol. 64, No. 1, Winter 2011.

activities. The PLAN has replenished its Gulf of Aden patrols chiefly in Djibouti, Oman, and Yemen.[170] To date, China has shown remarkably little interest in overseas naval-basing, echoing Beijing's longstanding resistance to overseas military-basing more generally. Further, both the replenishment ports themselves and the political risk of wartime operations, given host country considerations and vulnerability, mark a wide distance between limited peacetime replenishment contracts and the robust naval-basing requirements for wartime power projection.[171] Such basing requirements would at least include reasonably assured wartime access, deep-draft naval-pierside support, repair and rearmament facilities, prepositioning of wartime stocks, and shore-based aviation support, none of which is currently being pursued by China or by the host countries involved.

Protecting Chinese Citizens and Assets

The growth in overseas Chinese citizens and assets has outpaced the PLA's power projection capabilities and near-term ambitions.[172] China's citizens in Africa can be envisioned in three major communities, facing different security threats. The first group consists of officials associated with embassies and state-owned companies; these people often stay in an African state for a few years before moving to other foreign states, similar to their Western counterparts. Second are Chinese laborers brought in for major infrastructure projects; they tend to live in Chinese enclaves, interact little with the local population, and return to China upon project completion. Finally, there are private Chinese citizens and small-business owners who have expatriated to Africa, have little contact with the Chinese government, and are building their businesses in local markets, farms, or small-scale productions.[173] Laborers—and, to a lesser extent, officials—face threats from terrorist groups (such as the Movement for the Emancipation of the Niger

---

[170] Erickson, 2013.

[171] Kostecka, 2011.

[172] Andrew Scobell and Andrew J. Nathan, "China's Overstretched Military," *The Washington Quarterly*, Fall 2012.

[173] Shinn and Brown, 2012.

Delta, Boko Haram, and Al Qaeda in the Islamic Maghreb) targeting large projects for ransom or political effect. Small-business owners face some level of threat from terrorist groups but are more vulnerable to popular anger, given their close interaction with local populations and relative lack of organized security.[174]

Private Chinese security firms provide the majority of protection to larger overseas facilities; there are growing Chinese concerns about whether the quantity and quality of these guards are sufficient.[175] Threats to Chinese citizens exist in several areas across the continent. Nine Chinese energy-firm personnel were killed in Ethiopia in 2007, and in January of 2012, two kidnappings totaling more than 50 Chinese citizens occurred in Sudan and Egypt, killing one.[176] At least seven Chinese citizens were killed in northern Nigeria in several incidents in late 2012, including at least one killed by Boko Haram.[177] Zambian coal miners killed their Chinese manager during a riot over wages in August 2012, at a mine that the Zambian government seized in February 2013 for its poor safety record.[178] At present, the security of Chinese citizens in Africa has not been a large-scale domestic Chi-

---

[174] For an excellent portrayal of different Chinese communities' interactions with Tanzania, see the documentary film *When China Met Africa*, 2011.

[175] See the comments of Fu Shen, a manager of the Beijing Security Service General Company (The Jamestown Foundation, *China Brief*, Vol. 12, No. 10, May 11, 2012, p. 15). The company is allegedly founded and managed by former People's Armed Police officers. See also Xu Wei, "More Consideration Given to Guards for Overseas Workers," *China Daily*, February 22, 2012; and Yang Mian and Song Fei, "Further Reminding the Chinese Enterprises and Workforces in Africa of the Risks and Necessary Safety Measures," *Asia and Africa Review*, Vol. 2, 2012.

[176] Ford, 2012; Al Jazeera, "Kidnapped Chinese Workers Freed in Sudan," *Al Jazeera English*, February 7, 2012.

[177] Xinhua, "Two Killed in Northern Nigeria," *China Daily*, October 8, 2012d; Xinhua, "Chinese Killed by Boko Haram Suspects in Nigeria," *China Daily*, October 9, 2012e; Xinhua, "One Chinese Worker Shot Dead in Northern Nigeria," *China Daily*, October 20, 2012f; Xinhua, "At Least 4 Killed, Several Injured in Northern Nigeria Church Explosion," *NZWeek*, October 28, 2012g.

[178] BBC, "Zambian Miners Kill Chinese Manager During Pay Protest," August 5, 2012; Palash Ghost, "Zambia Seizes Chinese-Owned Mine Over Poor Safety Record: The Fraying Relations Between Beijing And Africa," *International Business Times*, February 21, 2013.

nese political issue. Should Beijing decide a more robust approach or rescue option is desirable, however, there are few regional PLA capabilities that could be readily deployed. There are probably Chinese special operations forces aboard the Gulf of Aden deployment, but it would be more difficult politically for them to become involved in a land-based contingency than to support China's antipiracy contribution in international waters. Further still, should moderate- to large-scale PLA assistance be needed in a NEO, the number of citizens and assets requiring protection dwarfs current PLA capabilities, particularly on anything less than a lengthy time frame.

The 2011 Libya Noncombatant Evacuation Operation: Another Notable First for the PLA

In reaction to rapidly deteriorating security in Libya during February 2011, the PLA played its largest role to date in a NEO of Chinese citizens abroad. The Libya NEO is not the first citizen evacuation conducted by the CCP; at least 12 overseas evacuations have occurred since 1990. Typically, such evacuations are led by the Chinese embassy and Ministry of Foreign Affairs, using commercial transportation as the primary option, echoing the methods of most foreign embassies. The PLA's participation in the 2011 Libya NEO was marginal: The majority of the 35,000 Chinese citizens were removed by commercial air and sea transportation chartered by regional CCP embassies. Four PLA Air Force Il-76 transports moved 1,700 citizens, routing from Xinjiang in Western China through Khartoum to Sabha in eastern Libya. The PLA Air Force then conducted more than 40 sorties to move the Chinese citizens (and more than 200 Nepalese citizens) to Khartoum.[179] The operation is the longest-range PLA Air Force operation known to date.[180] The PLAN also moved one of its most modern guided missile frigates (054A Jiangkai-II FFG *Xuzhou*) from the Gulf of Aden deployment, arriving on the final day to escort chartered civilian ships evac-

---

[179] Erickson, 2013.

[180] Gabe Collins and Andrew Erickson, "The PLA Air Force's First Overseas Operational Deployment," *China Signpost*, March 1, 2011.

uating Chinese citizens.[181] Despite its relatively small role, the NEO remains the most significant overseas PLA operation to date, and its successful organization and execution on relatively short notice is noteworthy of evolving PLA capabilities and multiagency coordination.

2012 and 2013 PLA Deployments to Mali and South Sudan: Illustrating the PLA's Evolving Role

In 2012 and 2013, PLA ground units saw historically significant deployments in support of U.N. peacekeeping operations. In January 2012, the PLA deployed its first overseas combat troops in support of peacekeeping operations—a "guard" force of about 50 PLA infantry to UNMISS. This force's mission was limited to force protection for PLA engineer and medical forces contributing to UNMISS, which Beijing argued were underprotected by existing U.N. elements. The detachment was part of the PLA's elite 162nd Motorized Infantry Division, whose last operational experience was in the 1989 clearing of Tiananmen Square.[182] In late December 2013, with the domestic civil conflict in South Sudan continuing to escalate, the U.N. Security Council agreed to double the size of UNMISS. It is unclear at present what new roles the PLA will take on in this expansion, but Beijing has committed to resending its special envoy for African affairs to Juba to meet with the conflicting parties.[183]

In July 2013, Beijing committed 395 peacekeepers to the U.N. Mission in Mali (MINUSMA), including a more significant infantry component.[184] MINUSMA is taking over from the African-led inter-

---

[181] Lili Zhang, "An Analysis of China's All-Out Efforts to Evacuate Chinese Nationals from Libya," *Contemporary World*, April 5, 2011. This journal is published by the International Liaison Department of the Central Committee of the Chinese Communist Party.

[182] Daniel Hartnett, "China's First Deployment of Combat Forces to a UN Peacekeeping Mission–South Sudan," Washington, D.C.: U.S.-China Economic and Security Review Commission, Staff Memo, March 13, 2012.

[183] BBC, "South Sudan Crisis: East Africa Would Not Accept Coup," December 27, 2013b; Waakhe Simon Wudu, "UN Speeds up Deployment as Fighting Rages in S. Sudan," *The Daily Star* (Lebanon), December 27, 2013.

[184] Xinhua, "135 Chinese Peacekeepers Arrive in Capital of Mali," *CRIEnglish*, December 5, 2013a; DefenceWeb, "Chinese Peacekeepers Arrive in Mali in Historic Deployment," December 11, 2013.

national support mission in Mali, coordinated by the Economic Community of West African States following the ouster of Islamic militants from northern Mali. In contrast to the guard force deployed to South Sudan, the PLA contingent to MINUSMA includes what Chinese statements call a "security force" of PLA infantry. The security force's mission will not be limited to protecting other PLA forces but instead will protect "MINUSMA headquarters and the living areas of peacekeeping forces" in Bamako.[185] The infantry are reportedly drawn from China's northeastern Shenyang military region, bordering North Korea and Russia—areas of obvious importance to the PLA Ground Force. The initial elements of this force arrived in early December 2013, consisting of 35 infantry, 35 engineers, and 65 medical staff.[186] The PLA contingent may face a more robust threat in their Mali deployment; a mid-December 2013 car bomb killed two Senegalese U.N. peacekeepers and injured seven in Mali's restive northeast.[187]

The 2012 and 2013 deployments mark milestones in the growth of China's contribution to U.N. peacekeeping operations. These exist among a series of such milestones, which taken together illustrate Beijing's evolving calculus: initially opposing such operations or interventions, first participating in 1999, increasing PLA participation over the next decade, beginning to include civilian police (rather than strictly noncombat troops) in 2004, and deploying its first infantry support in 2012 and 2013. Beijing has downplayed the significance of both infantry deployments, stressing that they fall within the U.N. mandate, were requested by the host country, and comply with China's policies of nonintervention.[188] Both deployments have been welcomed by the U.N. head of peacekeeping operations.[189]

---

[185] Murray, 2013.

[186] Xinhua, 2013a; DefenceWeb, 2013.

[187] Xinhua, "UN Slams Deadly Attack on Peacekeepers in Mali," December 15, 2013b.

[188] Murray, 2013.

[189] Xinhua, 2013a.

Potential Near- and Medium-Term Changes in Sino-African Relations

This section considers the near- and medium-term changes to Sino-African relations across the economic, political, and security domains.

Economic Relations

While growth in the Sino-African economic relationship is likely to continue, the rate of growth is likely to slow. The explosive growth of the past ten years was, to a large degree, the immediate reaction to China's "Go Global" economic policy, which partnered CCP support with exporting firms in order to encourage FDI and other investment. Growth rates stemming from this investment push will slow once markets react to the new sources of Chinese finance and eventually reach new equilibria. The Chinese economy itself is likely to encounter structurally slowing growth rates—this has likely already begun—which in turn should moderate demand growth for African raw materials and investments. While robust growth likely will continue for another five to ten years, there is little reason to expect that the exponential growth seen since the millennium will continue.

Further, it is unclear what effect China's planned economic rebalancing may have on its African relations. Beijing seeks to move China gradually from an export-oriented to domestic consumption–oriented economic posture.[190] Its ability to do so, and the potential costs of a failed rebalancing, are unclear at present. A successful rebalancing implies continued growth in raw material imports. A more consumption-oriented Chinese economy may export marginally fewer consumer goods to Africa, and may be more interested in gradually conducting

---

[190] In addition to being explicitly mentioned in the most recent Five-Year Plan (People's Republic of China, 2011), public discussion by senior CCP leadership of the need to rebalance the Chinese economy and avoid export dependence date to at least 2006. See Jin Rong, "Nation Told to Bolster Domestic Consumption," *China Daily*, November 4, 2006; Xinhua, "CPC Sets Targets for 12th Five-Year Program," Information Office of the State Council and the China International Publishing Group, October 27, 2010; Bloomberg News, "China's Wen Blocked by Politics from Fixing 'Unstable' Economy," March 3, 2010; and Yasheng Huang, "China's Great Rebalancing: Promise and Peril," McKinsey and Company, June 2013.

more low-paying and environmentally hazardous production in African states. The development of shale resources could diminish Chinese demand for overseas oil and gas, yet barriers to developing Chinese shale appear substantial.[191]

With U.S. oil imports from Africa potentially poised to level or decrease due to domestic shale development, Chinese firms will likely continue to increase their share of African oil exports. China currently exists in relatively fringe areas of the African oil market, but as imports increase and firms mature, China will be heading into the more mainstream African producers.[192] This will put Chinese firms into commercial competition with American firms, as well as likely increase China's influence with oil-producing states. American media sources tend to unnecessarily politicize and securitize China's energy imports; as China moves into deeper relationships with core producers, this tension is likely to increase.

The more troublesome aspects of China's resource import contracts may moderate as China establishes relationships with the more established energy exporters, or as current exporters develop. China's tactics—such as its aid-for-trade policy, use of resource-backed loans, and firms' tendency to leverage corruption—perform more strongly in less developed states, such as Angola, than in more-established exporting markets, such as Brazil.[193] As African exporters' civil society and

---

[191] In particular, China's shale potential is found far from consuming areas, requiring infrastructure development. Price asymmetries favor imported liquefied natural gas rather than speculative interior development. Further, Chinese shale potential is located in geologically difficult circumstances, which domestic firms are poorly placed to address, and adequate foreign partnering conditions have yet to emerge. Finally, China's shale areas suffer from the same lack of water and proximity to agriculture that plague many coal-producing areas. Shale development is water-intensive and competes with agriculture for limited water supplies in areas already facing desertification. See Steven Lewis, "China's Maritime Disputes in the East and South China Seas," testimony before the U.S.-China Economic Security Review Commission, Washington, D.C., April 4, 2013.

[192] Mikkal Herberg, "China's Maritime Disputes in the East and South China Seas," testimony before the U.S.-China Economic Security Review Commission, Washington, D.C., January 26, 2012, pp. 80–84.

[193] Ana Alves, "China's Economic Statecraft," *Journal of Current Chinese Affairs*, Vol. 42, No. 1, 2013.

legal climate develop, or as China moves to exporting from core markets alongside international oil firms, more of China's energy dealings likely will be pressured to conform to international norms.

There is academic debate over whether the debt burden of African states to Chinese financial sources is ultimately sustainable.[194] As noted previously, Chinese loans often lack the scrutiny on sustainability applied to loans from OECD states, the IMF, and the World Bank. While China's aggregate trade with Africa has largely been balanced, there are several African countries running unsustainable trade deficits, with Ethiopia a prominent example.[195] From 2000 to 2009, Beijing canceled $2.8 billion in the accumulated debt of 35 states, although the majority appears to have been foreign aid loans, and the rate of cancellations appears to have slowed.[196] States without raw materials to offer China often have few products that can compete in Chinese markets, but they continue to consume Chinese imports and loans. This is not a state-backed strategy by Beijing to create debt; the vast majority of such loans are commercial, and Beijing is concerned about both loan default and being labeled an exploitative power. Beijing is taking some steps to address the underlying trade imbalances, such as lowering tariffs, but for some states, a more substantial reordering may be inevitable. Similarly, African governments are likely to try to benefit from Chinese imports and investments while shielding domestic production, to the extent possible. China will have to navigate how it deals with trade practices in African states, some of which will be protectionist. How China reorders these relationships, the degree to which

---

[194] For examples, see Brown, 2012, pp. 49–54; Reisen Helmut, *Is China Actually Helping Improve Debt Sustainability in Africa?* Policy Brief, Intergovernmental Group of Twenty-Four on International Monetary Affairs and Development, 2008; Chilufya Chileshe, *Chinese Debt, Aid and Trade: Opportunity or Threat for Zambia?* Occasional Paper, South African Institute of International Affairs, December 2010.

[195] Shinn and Brown, 2012, p. 7. See also Institute for Security Studies and the African Forum and Network on Debt and Development, *ISS Workshop Report: National Consultation on Mapping Chinese Development Assistance in Africa: An Analysis of the Experiences of Ethiopia*, Addis Ababa, Ethiopia, July 30, 2012.

[196] Shinn, David H., "China-Africa Relations: The Big Picture," *International Policy Digest*, December 6, 2011c.

Beijing can and will rein in competitive exporters, and how China deals with issues of African insolvency will affect China's African and international reputation. Further, as noted previously, should the debt burdens prove unsustainable and African states require debt restructuring, such restructuring could easily fall on OECD states or the IMF.

Political Factors

China's growing African interests will complicate its ability to remain agnostic about the internal affairs of African states. While rhetorically long committed to African states' interests, such commitment was easier in previous decades when levels of interaction and conflicting interests were low. Presently, tension between China's competing interests in Africa is manageable. China may in fact be in a "sweet spot" in its African relations, where economic incentives have taken effect but serious conflicting interests have yet to emerge. As China becomes more deeply involved, Beijing may wrestle with how to define its relations to African states as its growing interests conflict with those of host countries. It is currently espousing diplomatic and rhetorical positions, such as noninterference, that were created when Beijing was distant from African affairs and wanted to critique the involvement of foreign powers. Now being involved, these diplomatic and political stances appear under increased tension.

At root are fundamental questions about the direction of Beijing's approach to African states' domestic issues, dedication to host-country sovereignty, and diplomatic skill. Several current examples outside Africa suggest that Beijing faces a challenging future. In contrast to its rhetoric of developing state solidarity, China has not been apolitical to developing states in its immediate periphery, most notably in Southeast Asia, where regional interests conflict significantly. While the geopolitical circumstances are decidedly different, Chinese Foreign Minister Yang Jiechi's comments to the Association of Southeast Asian Nations that "China is a big country and other countries are small countries, and that's just a fact" suggests that there are limits to Chinese solidarity with developing states when interests contradict.[197] Certainly in South-

---

[197] Terry McCarthy, "China's Aggressive Stance Reveals Lack of Coordination," *Yale Global*, December 5, 2012.

east Asia, China has territorial and sovereignty issues that are absent from its relations in Africa, and Chinese relations with Southeast Asian nations are therefore not a direct analogue to its relations with developing states writ large. These disputes (and Yang's rationale) do, however, suggest that there is potential risk of Chinese exceptionalism and great-power hubris in its future dealings with developing states in situations where Chinese rhetoric and interests are in conflict. Such an approach by Beijing would risk supporting an image that Chinese nonintervention is selectively self-serving rather than a principled respect for other states' sovereignty. This is not to imply that China's position toward developing countries is insincere or novel (for example, some of U.S. President Lyndon Johnson's characterizations of South Vietnam were similar to Yang's comments).[198] It instead suggests that Beijing's stance toward African states will be more complicated as Chinese interests and power continue to expand.

The tension between growing interests and nonintervention is unlikely to be limited to bilateral relations. As China's African presence grows, both African publics and the international community will likely expect more from China. Domestic Chinese stakeholders involved in Africa similarly may also expect more from Beijing. All of these actors are likely to have less appetite for Beijing dealing with African problems in an agnostic manner. Such tension can be seen currently in China's arms exports, which are increasingly difficult to describe as responsible commercial activity distinct from the political realm. Similarly, should China enter more deeply into a subset of African states' political issues to protect or advance its own interests, this will call into question claims of principled nonintervention in other cases where China chooses not to become involved.

Beijing will also likely have to navigate the issue of scapegoating. As noted earlier, China's rising presence over the past decade has generated some populist anti-Chinese political tensions. To date, these have centered primarily on Chinese merchants displacing African merchants in local markets, or on Chinese labor and safety practices.

---

[198] Frank E. Vandiver, *Shadows of Vietnam: Lyndon Johnson's Wars*, College Station, Tex.: Texas A&M University Press, 1997, Chapter One.

Four states have recently passed laws curtailing the presence of foreigners in markets, targeting the growing Chinese presence. In each case, the Chinese embassies involved supported the host countries' right to set and enforce their own laws.[199] In June 2013, 166 Chinese citizens were detained and expelled from Ghana over allegations of illegal gold mining there.[200] China's presence will continue to grow as a sensitive domestic political issue in African states. As populist movements demonize (often unfairly) the Chinese presence for domestic political gain, it likely will become increasingly difficult for Beijing to ignore such African voices. Further, such scapegoating can exacerbate security issues facing Chinese citizens and firms. This may be in part ameliorated by the growing savvy of Chinese actors in Africa, as the first generation of African-born Chinese reduces the current cultural gap between communities. However, like the Western powers, the fundamental power asymmetries between China and its African partners will likely make it an increasing target for anticolonial rhetoric.

In both the political and economic realms, Beijing likely will have to manage a proliferation of substate Chinese actors, particularly overseas firms and Chinese citizens living in Africa. These actors' interests will not perfectly align with Beijing's, nor will their activities be transparent to government oversight. As stated previously, China has struggled with transparency and control issues domestically, as well as with overseas firms. While Beijing can often impose ad-hoc control over a given issue at a given time, the underfunctioning CCP bureaucracy has not been able to manage most sectors independent of senior leadership, which simply cannot manage all affairs at all times.[201] This

[199] The four states are Kenya, Malawi, Nigeria, and Uganda. The Uganda case reportedly saw violence between locals and Chinese merchants. See *Oxford Analytica*, "New Challenges Arise as China-Africa Ties Deepen," January 2013.

[200] Bloomberg News, "China's Africa Role Under New Scrutiny as Miners Expelled," June 7, 2013.

[201] While many Western media sources envision a monolithic state with control over subordinate political and economic actors, Beijing struggles for a well-documented lack of control over local governments, SOEs, and private interests. See Starr, 2001; Lieberthal and Lampton, 1992; Shirk, 2007; Downs, 2008, 2009; and Mertha, 2009, for accessible descriptions.

lack of central control is not a new issue for Beijing; the traditional Chinese saying "mountains high, emperor far" (山高王远) stems from the historical difficulty in the imperial past of the central government's control of China's immense population and territory. The disaggregation trend is particularly acute in Africa, aided by distance and the relative lack of consistent oversight from some African governments. China's private-sector and local government-owned interests are growing quickly in Africa. The activities of these actors may increase the tension that China faces among its foreign policy goals, relations with African states, and popular pressure to support Chinese citizens abroad.

Security Issues

China faces several emerging security challenges related to its evolving interests in Africa. The initiation of the 2008 Gulf of Aden patrol and 2011 Libya NEO were milestones for both the CCP and PLA and mark the initial steps in China's effort to manage new security problems with limited power projection capability.[202] The severity of China's security issues in Africa, the extent of PLA capabilities to answer these, and the strategic direction defined by CCP leadership are likely to change, although such changes will most likely be gradual. The dwindling and eventual stoppage in 2012 of oil trade from the Sudans illustrates the risks that China incurs by investing in dangerous areas. In terms of future threats, as Ely Ratner has argued, China is likely to face sensitive state failures, overtly anti-Chinese popular movements, terrorism, and kidnappings with increased frequency.[203] Beijing's conception of its security interests has continued to grow, best indicated by the 2004 introduction of "New Historic Missions" (新的历史使命) for the PLA that highlight China's expanding global interests and the need for "safeguarding world peace and promoting common development."[204] Nontraditional security threats have grown in Chinese security discourse, including in the CCP's 2006 Africa

[202] Nathan and Scobell, 2012; Mulvenon, 2009.

[203] Ratner, 2011.

[204] Cortez A. Cooper, *The PLA Navy's "New Historic Missions," Expanding Capabilities for a Re-Emergent Maritime Power*, Santa Monica, Calif.: RAND Corporation, CT-332, 2009.

White Paper: "In order to enhance the ability of both sides to address nontraditional security threats, it is necessary to increase intelligence exchange, [and] explore more effective ways and means for closer cooperation in combating terrorism, small-arms smuggling, drug trafficking, transnational economic crimes, etc."[205] China's 2013 Defense White Paper devotes an unprecedented three full paragraphs to protecting China's overseas interests.[206] Significant mismanagement of security crises in Africa could put Beijing's domestic legitimacy and its principles of foreign noninterference into conflict. This could potentially force Beijing to compromise on noninterference and could incentivize improvements in the PLA's distant capabilities.

China has relied on African governments and militia, the Ministry of Foreign Affairs, and private security contractors to protect Chinese citizens; these may not be sufficient to answer future threats. China will likely find it must increasingly assert itself to protect its growing interests. As former Ambassador David H. Shinn has pointed out, African states themselves may pressure Beijing to increase its security commitment to areas in which it has invested heavily.[207] Given that it can be perceived as allied to several repressive regimes, China may become more of a target for opposition, rebel, or terrorist movements. A future China may wish to secure either an embassy or an overseas commercial asset in a country abroad facing rapidly deteriorating stability, terrorist threats, or violent anti-Chinese demonstrations. Perhaps partly in recognition of this kind of potential, recent PRC defense white papers have been less stringent in emphasizing noninterference. While Chinese political and diplomatic sources and statements continue to stress noninterference in African affairs, the last white paper to explicitly cite nonintervention overseas was in 2000. China's operational definition of *noninterference* has already evolved to meet Beijing's strategic calculus; for example, China previously criticized U.N. peacekeeping

---

[205] People's Republic of China, 2006.

[206] IOSC, 2013a.

[207] Shinn and Eisenman, 2012, p. 372.

deployments as violating sovereignty before becoming a major participant.[208] Further adaptations are likely, if difficult to predict precisely.

While the 2011 Libya NEO marked an operational milestone for the PLA, it may be a sign of emerging and operationally difficult requirements. The successful execution of the NEO, while not requiring a great deal of PLA support, may create an expectation in the Chinese public that the CCP protect or evacuate Chinese citizens in future scenarios. It is not difficult to imagine, however, Chinese NEOs under much more difficult circumstances. As demonstrated most recently in the Arab Spring, instability can occur quickly and be difficult to predict. Further, instability in countries such as Chad, the DRC, Nigeria, and Zimbabwe could present access problems that dwarf the difficulties presented in coastal Libya.

Large changes to China's security posture in Africa are speculative and not likely in the next decade. However, given growing interests, it is possible that China could attempt to create a minimally invasive capability for reacting to crises in Africa. Such an initial capability could combine several medium-term developments. The Gulf of Aden deployment has revealed the difficulties of extended PLAN operations at a long distance from mainland sustainment. While such discussion is relatively nascent, some Chinese security sources have called for permanent assured access to African ports to facilitate future operations.[209] As detailed previously, this is distinct from any conception of naval-basing but could better facilitate peacetime replenishment. The PLA could wish to create closer and more-permanent options for fixed- or rotary-wing aviation; such a capability would assist with responses

---

[208] Kostecka, 2011.

[209] For example, the Seychelles has reportedly offered a more permanent replenishment arrangement for the PLAN, which the CCP has correctly emphasized is not commensurate with an overseas base. For an exploration of the meaningful differences between a peacetime replenishment site and a naval base, and the potential for Chinese replenishment sites in the Indian Ocean, see Kostecka, 2011. For the Seychelles discussion, see Li Xiaokun, "Navy Looks at Offer from Seychelles," *China Daily*, December 13, 2013; Mandip Singh, "China Base a Threat to India Navy?" *The Diplomat*, December 17, 2011; and Maseeh Rahman, "Chinese Plans in Seychelles Revive Indian Fears of Encirclement," *The Guardian*, March 23, 2012.

to NEOs and humanitarian assistance and disaster relief missions. This could be combined with special operations, or a deployable site-security team akin to the U.S. Marine Corps' Fleet Antiterrorism Security Team, to protect threatened facilities or people. Beijing also could consider becoming involved in countering domestic instability in key states where its interests are threatened. Such a capability could include security assistance, training, or deployment of the PLA law enforcement (People's Armed Police) to buoy partner government capabilities. A country facing instability that has deeper political relations with Beijing, such as Sudan or Zimbabwe, would be the most likely candidate for Chinese intervention. In such a scenario, an invitation for PLA participation would minimize political fallout and Beijing's tensions over noninterference. In any case, the location of such assets and capabilities within Africa is an open question. China's distributed interests in Africa, and the difficulties of distance and access, highlight the operational costs of Beijing's political resistance to overseas basing. Some voices within the PLA have begun to call for a reinvestigation of China's no-bases position.[210]

---

[210] For a brief synopsis of indicators of debate within the CCP over foreign-basing, see Kostecka, 2011, pp. 61–64.

CHAPTER FOUR

Sino-American Interest Correlation in Africa and Conclusions

This chapter examines the common, competing, and conflicting interests of American and Chinese actors in Africa before concluding with recommendations for U.S. policy.

Conflict and Commonality Between U.S. and Chinese Interests in Africa

Drawn from a range of government and academic sources, U.S. strategic interests in Africa are defined here as stability; democratic and constitution-based governance; judicial and human rights improvements; African economic growth; increased trade (including natural resources) and access to African markets; defeating transnational terrorist, criminal, and extremist groups; and access to military operating locations and overflight rights when needed.[1]

Common Interests

The United States and China share a fundamental interest in the stability of African states. African stability is a prerequisite for the economic

[1] David H. Shinn, "China's Growing Role in Africa: Implications for U.S. Policy," testimony before the Senate Committee on Foreign Relations Subcommittee on African Affairs, November 1, 2011b; Walter H. Kansteiner III and J. Stephen Morrison, *Rising U.S. Stakes in Africa: Seven Proposals to Strengthen U.S.-Africa Policy*, Washington, D.C.: Center for Strategic and International Studies, Report of the Africa Policy Advisory Panel, May 2004; and Ian Taylor, *The International Relations of Sub-Saharan Africa*, New York: Continuum, 2010.

benefits that both states seek in African relations, as well as the deepening relationships, stable diplomatic support, and global leadership image that each hopes to portray. Neither state has fundamental political concerns or mercantilist economic aims that would cause it to seek widespread regime changes. The conflicts that have been frequent in parts of Africa interfere with both states' interests, because the resulting instability precludes development, prevents deep bilateral relations, raises doubts about international leadership, and often portends instability in bordering states. Relatedly, both states share an interest, which is likely to grow, in defeating violent extremists and cross-border criminal networks. The United States has been far more active in countering these threats to date. Yet, as stated previously, transnational groups are beginning to specifically target overseas Chinese citizens and facilities. As Chinese interests, presence, and investments in Africa grow, networks that degrade stability broadly, and target Chinese interests specifically, will become increasingly difficult for Beijing to ignore. China's 2006 White Paper on Africa highlights transnational terrorist and criminal threats as a concern requiring increased attention.[2]

Similarly, both states seek growing African economies and improvements in the African infrastructure needed to facilitate trade and investment, and economic improvement is strongly correlated to both states' interest in African stability. Such improvements also facilitate the efficient and economical production of Africa's natural resources. Growing African economies and functioning infrastructure create stronger African markets for the consumption of exports from both states. Finally, African economic growth highlights the positive role and reputation for both states while easing their interactions with new African partners.

Competing Interests

The United States and China have several competing commercial and diplomatic interests in Africa. Both states desire access to Africa's petroleum and natural resources. Such commercial competition exists between the United States and other states as well, including the United

---

2 People's Republic of China, 2006.

Kingdom and France, and need not be a source of bilateral Sino-American tension. Both states would like to export more to Africa; while the United States has been relatively cool on Africa as an export market, this may change if African states' GDP growth continues apace. However, at present, the United States and China tend to operate in different industries and sectors, rather than being in direct commercial competition.[3] Finally, both states seek political support from African states for their wider public diplomatic goals, benefiting from African votes in bodies like the United Nations and WTO. Such competition also exists between the United States and other states, and need not represent a highly-charged or zero-sum source of bilateral competition.

Tensions surrounding commercial competition in Africa can be heightened by U.S. perceptions of alleged Chinese cheating in economic interactions. In evaluating Chinese economic activity, it should be remembered that both states use policy banks to assist exporting businesses, China does not have a private-sector alternative to heavy state involvement, and the difference between the United States and China in politicizing economic ties is a matter of degree rather than pure dichotomy. Still, the means by which China sometimes packages state support and commercial activity would be against OECD rules, and Chinese firms are generally less scrutinized than U.S. firms bound by the Foreign Corrupt Practices Act.[4] China's state-centric economic structure and abundant currency reserves have allowed SOEs—and, to a lesser extent, private Chinese enterprises—access to investment capital that market dynamics alone would not favor. This has allowed some Chinese firms to pay more than the likely market price for assets or access, or to package concessionary loans with the stipulation that they involve Chinese firms and Chinese sources. Further, China's state-capitalism model gives political leaders the ability to commit capital and trade in much larger quantities than economies oriented more toward free markets. However, as described in Chapter Three, the large role of the Chinese state in its economic structure creates challenges as well as opportunities.

---

[3] GAO, 2013.

[4] Brown, 2012, pp. 74–75.

As noted, the scope and geostrategic bent of CCP support to its firms, however, is often overstated. Most Chinese commercial activity succeeds on its own merits, particularly in China's exports to Africa. Moreover, Chinese and U.S. firms are frequently pursuing different projects in different African states, particularly with respect to petroleum. A larger state role in firms' commercial decisions, however, brings both benefits and costs. While China does not play by the rules of the OECD, neither does it enjoy the benefits of membership. Deeper politicization of economic activity also creates inefficiencies and the poor choices associated with governments "picking winners" rather than allowing markets to function freely. For example, China has a history of overpaying for equity in overseas oil ventures.[5]

There is little credible potential for a Sino-American conflict over resources in Africa. Contrary to popular and perennial assumptions about resource wars, industry and energy analysis sources project adequate supply of conventional hydrocarbons beyond 2035.[6] Given reservoir depletion curves, any tightening of supply would be gradual. The adequacy of supply is further augmented when tertiary production and unconventional sources are considered (such as shale and tar sands). U.S. strength in unconventional sources, and potential energy independence, further reduces the likelihood of a conflict. Even in a future with vastly inflated hydrocarbon prices, these costs pale in comparison to those associated with a Sino-American war, the economic costs of which likely fall more heavily on China than the United States.[7] Global hydrocarbon resources are distributed via a fungible global market, with many stakeholders and moderate diversity of supply. This enables importing states to buy a predictable supply of hydrocarbons at

---

[5] Downs, 2004. See also Frederik Balfour, "A Global Shopping Spree for the Chinese—Mainland Companies Are Snapping up More Overseas Assets," *BusinessWeek*, November 18, 2002, p. 24; and *Petroleum Intelligence Weekly*, "Eager Chinese Pay Dearly for Foreign Assets," April 29, 2002.

[6] International Energy Agency, 2012; BP, *BP Statistical Review of World Energy*, June 2012.

[7] RAND interviews with senior financial industry executives, May–August 2013. Please contact the author or RAND for a list of interviews. For a fascinating overview of Sino-American economic vulnerabilities, see Markus Jaegar, *Sino-U.S. Relations: Economic Deterrence and Asymmetric Vulnerability*, Deutsche Bank Research, 2010.

reasonable and competing prices over long contracts. African sources do not constitute a majority of this supply chain, and supposed victory in a theoretical great-power resource war would not guarantee security of resource supply. In sum, the potential for either China or the United States to be willing to enter war with a nuclear adversary over African oil, let alone other, less valuable resources, is extraordinarily small.[8]

China's hydrocarbon investment and development in Africa does not threaten U.S. or global energy security. On the contrary, as industry and academic sources have highlighted and as described in Chapter Three, its investment and development increase hydrocarbon availability for all consuming states.[9] Because oil trades in a fungible global market, creating additional supply from new Chinese investments in Africa adds to the aggregate global supply. Each barrel of oil that China acquires in new African production is a barrel that it is not buying from the global supply pool. As stated previously, a large portion (likely the majority) of Chinese-owned production in Africa is sold on to global markets rather than returned to China.[10] The most potent threat to global energy security, as identified by the OECD's International Energy Agency, among others, is a lack of adequate investment in exploration and production.[11] Chinese investment, particularly on the fringes of the African oil market where the OECD states have been absent, adds to global energy security by bringing additional supply to market. Perennial arguments surrounding "peak oil" and "resource

---

[8] Control of resources can generate conflict in smaller states (as demonstrated in the Sudans), as regional actors fight for control over production. In smaller conflicts over regional geography, resources are not fungible: There are a limited number of viable areas, which are either controlled by one party or split between them. For major consuming states in a global market, however, the potential for controlling resource supply is different for a host of political and economic reasons. In small resource conflicts over production, winning is possible. Consuming states, however, cannot dominate a market in resource supply to the disadvantage of other players.

[9] Herberg, 2012, pp. 80–84; Downs, 2007, pp. 42–68; and Lewis, 2013.

[10] See footnote 46 in Chapter Three, on equity oil.

[11] International Energy Agency, 2012; BP, 2012.

conflict" mask the reality of Chinese energy activities in Africa and contribute to unnecessary tension and politicization.[12]

Conflicting Interests

Unlike the Cold War, when geopolitical tensions in Africa between the democratic West and Communist bloc were shaped by essentially irreconcilable ideologies, contemporary Sino-American interests in Africa are far less divergent and less dangerous. First, as covered above, the differences in Chinese and American interests are less diametrically opposed, with substantial interest overlap in African political stability, steady imports of natural resources, and increasing markets for exports. Beijing has not espoused a radically divergent ideology, attempted to reignite communism, or attempted to create opposed spheres of influence in Africa. As such, contemporary Sino-American disagreements in Africa are far less zero-sum than they were during the Cold War. Further, disagreements over governance, human rights, and international norms in Africa (see below) are far less critical to both states' security and economic access than their Cold War analogues. Put simply, Cold War geopolitics are a poor model for understanding contemporary Sino-American interest correlation in Africa. United States and Chinese interests diverge most seriously over the role of foreign powers in supporting good governance and international human rights norms in Africa. The United States emphasizes free-market mechanisms, constitutionally constrained democratic government, cultivation of civil society, and adherence to international human rights norms, both generally and in Africa. In the U.S. view, China's politicized economic ties to Africa have undermined good governance, contributed to authoritarianism, and delayed African political development.[13] China has emphasized apolitical economic ties, largely eschewing human rights issues, and openly criticized what it deems foreign interference. Not surprisingly, given their domestic contexts, U.S. and Chinese media tend to disagree about the role of foreign states in economic development. Chi-

[12] For an interesting discussion of China and the perennial arguments concerning resource wars, see David Victor, "What Resource Wars?" *The National Interest,* December 2007.

[13] See Brautigam, 2009.

nese sources tend to argue meaningful development proceeds from foreign economic investment and political noninterference, while American sources tend to argue the need for broader political and economic development measures pursued jointly.[14] Chinese perspectives on the role of foreign states in political and economic development are likely shaped in part by China's historical experience. With regard to political development, foreign powers played a large role in China's disintegration during the nineteenth and early twentieth centuries. With regard to economics, for all of the significant social and economic costs associated with Maoist rule, Chinese economic models demonstrated successful state-led development and industrialization for a poor agrarian economy.

The conflicting views over norms are most acute on issues surrounding so-called pariah African states. Chinese investment, particularly in the face of sanctions by other economic powers, has insulated such states as Sudan and Zimbabwe from Western and U.S. pressure. This has blunted the effectiveness of sanctions, part of a wider pattern of tension over relations with pariah states that includes Chinese relations with Iran and North Korea.

Conclusions and Recommendations

View China's African Relations in Their Proper Context

It is difficult to confidently measure China's aggregate effect on African states' political and civil society norms. It appears that the positive effects of Chinese investment in African economies and infrastructure has produced greater benefits for African stability and prosperity than the negative effects of Beijing's opposition to Western political norms and displacement of some indigenous industries. China's abundant for-

[14] Both states' arguments have plausible support within development economics literature. Academic sources point to the fragility of economic development without political liberalization, while others argue that political liberalization before reaching a per-capita-income threshold breeds instability. More importantly, Sino-American disagreements on development and political liberalism are rooted in deeper normative beliefs stemming from each state's domestic political culture, history, economies, and international relations.

eign currency reserves, long-term view, and comparative appetite for risk have allowed it to invest in African economies and market sectors that were previously ignored. A study by Canadian economists estimated that Chinese outgoing investment alone accounted for "a significant, even if in some cases small, portion of the elevated growth in Sub-Saharan Africa" seen from 2005 to 2009, despite the intervening global financial crisis.[15] More specifically, China's financial depth and singular relationship also allowed for more than $13 billion of investment in Angolan infrastructure shortly after Angola's civil war—investments that Western banks would have been loath to make due to risk of default—which contributed to Angolan recovery and stability.[16]

China's unfavorable activities in Africa should be kept in perspective. U.S. and Chinese critics both tend to compare an idealized version of their own nation's involvement in Africa with a selective criticism of the other's activities. While Chinese firms have violated local laws and international expectations, many states have struggled with corrupt and amoral practices from their firms in Africa. The Chinese have no more dealt only with autocracies than the United States has dealt only with democracies. Many states' firms, including European partners, have undercut sanctions in order to support their interests without similar fanfare.[17] Given that China is only one nation in a larger phenomenon of growing interaction between BRIC countries and African economies, singling out Chinese economic interactions appears more suspect. Many states feature a heavy state role in their political economies, and state-owned firms from India and Brazil have undertaken international business practices similar to China's (though

---

15 Aaron Weisbrod and John Whalley, "The Contribution of Chinese FDI to Africa's Pre Crisis Growth Surge," National Bureau of Economic Research Working Paper 17544, October 2011, p. 2.

16 Shinn and Brown, 2012, p. 6.

17 For example, U.N. sanctions on Iraq during the 1990s (Paul Heaton, "Oil for What?—Illicit Iraqi Oil Contracts and the U.N. Security Council," *Journal of Economic Perspectives*, Vol. 19, No. 4, 2005). See also Brent J. Talbot, "The Transatlantic Gap over Iraq," *European Security*, Vol. 17, No. 1, 2008.

not at the same scale) without similar scrutiny and politicization.[18] Further, China is not the only investor in pariah states; Indian and Malaysian firms have also invested heavily in Sudan's oil sector, for example.[19] Despite Equatorial Guinea being one of the most corrupt and human rights abusing regimes in Africa, the United States is heavily involved in its oil sector, with the U.S. State Department noting, "U.S. oil companies are one of Equatorial Guinea's largest investors, and they have a lead role in oil and gas exploration and extraction."[20]

The United States and OECD states clearly give more weight to human rights and good governance in Africa than China does. Yet China's more problematic political and economic activities in Africa are not nefarious; instead, they reflect Chinese actors' relative lack of oversight, myopia regarding economic growth, preference for expediency, and lack of comfort with established multilateral economic institutions. Chinese firms arguably have taken advantage of the open system and debt salience generated primarily by the ties between African states and international economic institutions (primarily the IMF, World Bank, and OECD), without sufficient heed to the broader consequences. As discussed in the sections about economic and future trends, this type of "free-riding" generates resentment on the part of Western actors and, more importantly, threatens the debt sustainability

---

[18] Harry G. Broadman and Isik Gozde, *Africa's Silk Road: China and India's New Economic Frontier*, Washington, D.C.: World Bank, 2007; Barney Jopson, "BRICs in Africa: Adding It up," *Financial Times*, Beyond BRICs blog, August 5, 2010; Kimenyi, Mwangi Kimenyi, and Zenia Lewis, "The BRICs and the New Scramble for Africa," in *Foresight Africa: The Continent's Greatest Challenges and Opportunities for 2011*, Washington, D.C.: Brookings Institution, Africa Growth Initiative, 2011. For a more critical collection of essays, see Fantu Cheru and C. I. Obi, eds., *The Rise of China and India in Africa: Challenges, Opportunities and Critical Interventions*, London: Zed, 2010.

[19] U.S. Energy Information Administration, *Country Analysis Brief: Sudan and South Sudan*, Washington, D.C.: U.S. Department of Energy, September 5, 2013d.

[20] Adam Nossiter, "U.S. Engages with an Iron Leader in Equatorial Guinea," *New York Times*, May 30, 2011; U.S. Department of State, "U.S. Relations with Equatorial Guinea: Fact Sheet," Bureau of African Affairs, April 1, 2013; U.S. Department of State, "A Guide to the United States' History of Recognition, Diplomatic, and Consular Relations, by Country, Since 1776: Equatorial Guinea," Office of the Historian, undated; Voice of America, "U.S. to Open 'Mini Embassy' in Equatorial Guinea," November 19, 2002.

of some African states. However, U.S. statements comparing the worst of Chinese practices to the best of U.S. ideals suggests to Africans that American leaders are misinformed or ill-intentioned.

Similarly, the depth and effect of Sino-American disagreement over pariah states is often overstated. While China disagrees with the severity of approach and policy instruments employed by the West regarding pariah states, it shares the fundamental desire for stability in these countries and does not want their struggles to attract unflattering international attention toward China. It is not surprising, therefore, that Beijing itself has pressured pariah governments to conform, often in states where Western access and influence was weak. Most prominently, Beijing was instrumental in pressuring Khartoum into negotiations when its behavior regarding Darfur and South Sudan became too egregious.[21] Subsequently, in 2011 and 2012, Beijing was at the center of efforts to bring about negotiations between Sudan and newly independent South Sudan—unsurprisingly, given its economic interests in both states.[22] Neither has Chinese support been unconditional for pariah regimes, as demonstrated by cooling relations with Zimbabwe in recent years.[23]

This is not to argue that the United States should cease its support for international norms and accountable, democratic governance in Africa. Rather, it implies U.S. policymakers should be realistic about the extent to which these ideals are under threat and need to be directly defended. Struggles against authoritarianism and illiberalism in Africa, with decidedly mixed results, long predate China's new role on the continent. African states will choose their own destinies and will balance between Beijing and Washington. Attempting to force states to choose between a Washington and a Beijing consensus is unlikely to be successful, yet it can alienate both Beijing and African leaders.

---

[21] Robert I. Rotberg, ed., *China into Africa: Trade, Aid, and Influence*, Washington, D.C.: Brookings Institution, 2008, p. 13, pp. 259–270; Stephanie Kleine-Ahlbrandt and Andrew Small, "China's New Dictatorship Diplomacy: Is Beijing Parting with Pariahs?" *Foreign Affairs*, Vol. 87, No. 1, 2008.

[22] Brown, 2012.

[23] Kleine-Ahlbrandt and Small, 2008.

Instead, the United States can continue to support African civil society, rule of law, and transparent government where conditions allow. U.S. dedication to African governance, civil society, and well-being can be demonstrated without the need for direct and public comparisons to China (particularly inaccurate comparisons). Beijing should be pressured on the issues of arms sales and arms transparency, and it has shown some response to the international opprobrium resulting from such sales.[24] Because there are limitations to what China can offer Africa (see next section), African states are still likely to engage heavily with the United States and seek U.S. leadership in several areas. As argued below, the best defense against sliding international norms in Africa is a reinvigoration of U.S.-African ties, rather than a focus on bilateral competition with China.

Avoid Elevating Low-Level Competition to Bilateral Strategic Tension

China's African relationships are not a strategic threat to American interests in Africa. Unlike the Cold War, the United States and China share a fundamental interest in African stability and economic growth. Further, the two states lack directly opposed and irreconcilable political interests and ideologies. These factors argue for a more moderate American response. Beijing shows no interest in overthrowing governments, sponsoring substate groups, or spreading a radically divergent political or economic worldview. While natural commercial and diplomatic competition ensues, and Washington and Beijing disagree on international norms and democratic governance, the importance of these disagreements pales in comparison to the interests that both states have in stable Sino-American ties and African stability. A China that invests in pariah states and resists international human rights norms in Africa is not ideal, but it does not pose an exceptional threat to American interests. Finally, given the degree to which Beijing struggles to control its subordinate economic actors, the United States should resist the desire to divine Beijing's strategic intent from each action.

---

[24] Taylor, 2013, pp. 457–475, 468–470.

A balanced perspective will be difficult for both states to achieve, given the low levels of Sino-American trust. Chinese trust of U.S. intentions is low and likely resistant to improvement.[25] Unnecessarily competitive U.S. rhetoric and actions can feed these suspicions. Economically, Western media sources have regularly accused China of "pillaging" African resources,[26] despite the United States (and several other European countries) consuming far more African oil and having less balanced trade with African states over the past decade. Senior U.S. figures have echoed such sentiments; then–Secretary of State Clinton's 2011 insinuation of a Chinese "new colonialism in Africa," and the 2012 implication that China is monofocused on African resources while the United States "adds value, rather than extracts it," were considered inflammatory by the Chinese press.[27] As exemplified by China's attempt to purchase the American energy firm Unocal in 2005, politicization can prevent legitimate commerce and suggest faults in U.S. commitment to open markets, at the same time that the United States is attempting to convince China not to politicize its economic relations.[28] Similarly, Western media have greatly overstated the amount of concessional finance that China has engaged in within Africa. Within the security sphere, unease over China's contribution to port development and search for reliable naval refitting arrangements has launched a cottage industry around the "string of pearls" Chinese naval threat to the Indian Ocean.[29] Should the PLA expand in Africa in coming years, similarly unhelpful excitement is likely. Such zero-sum approaches and competitive rhetoric antagonize

---

[25] Kenneth Lieberthal and Jisi Wang, *Addressing U.S.-China Strategic Distrust*, Washington, D.C.: Brookings Institution, John L. Thornton China Center, 2012.

[26] Agence France-Presse, "Anthropologist Jane Goodall: China Is Pillaging Africa Like an Old Colonial Power," Raw Story, February 17, 2014.

[27] Wing, 2012; Associated Press in Beijing, "Chinese State Media Slam Hillary Clinton's Speech in Africa," *The Guardian*, August 3, 2012; Katrina Manson, "China Hits Back at Clinton's Africa Comments," *The Washington Post*, August 3, 2012; Reuters, 2011.

[28] Flynt Leverett and Jeffrey Bader, "Managing China U.S. Energy Competition in the Middle East," *The Washington Quarterly*, Vol. 29, No. 1, 2005.

[29] Kostecka, 2011.

China over secondary interests. They also suggest to Beijing that the United States holds different standards for China than other states and is indeed interested in containment, while suggesting to African states that U.S. relations are skewed toward balance-of-power politics rather than genuine partnership. Finally, such approaches increase the space for African states to play the United States and China off of one another, appealing to each state's strategic distrust and tendency to perceive geopolitical competition.[30]

Recognize That China's Approach to Africa is Likely to Be Resistant to Major Change

Sino-African relationships are based on economic foundations that are unlikely to change quickly. China's state-centric and sovereignty-focused approach to African states stems from the political economy of the Chinese state and Beijing's domestic interest in noninterference from outside powers. In terms of overlapping economic interests, China wants resources, markets, investment opportunities, and diplomatic support for noninterference. In exchange, it offers a large pool of financial capital with a high-risk threshold, a strong construction sector, and cheap manufactured goods. African states generally want investment and infrastructure, have inexpensive labor and/or resources, have consumers who enjoy Chinese products, and often share a desire for a nonintrusive international political environment. Such structural-level factors underpinning Sino-African relations make it likely that they will endure as long as these factors endure. U.S. rhetorical or political opposition to Sino-African relations will likely fail to be effective while alienating both regions.

Sino-American disagreement over international norms in Africa reflects both countries' domestic political structures, histories, and guiding philosophies. These positions are unlikely to change quickly. The U.S. perspective is that economic development without political liberalization brings social instability, which contradicts the CCP's domestic political vision of continuing to expand the economy while tightly controlling China's political life. Efforts to question the human rights

---

[30] David H. Shinn, 2011b.

norms of African states are indirectly threatening to Beijing, which does not wish for international scrutiny on its own domestic human rights issues. Even if policymakers accept these ideals as normatively correct, it is unrealistic to expect Beijing to spread international human rights norms in Africa that it does not embrace at home. Similarly, China's centralization of economic activity and curtailments of individual liberty contrast with the U.S. founding ideologies and its Cold War identity. Such differences are resistant to change and can trigger emotional responses.

Recognize the Limits of Chinese Influence

The growth in Chinese influence in Africa is not limitless. Western states, especially taken in aggregate, outweigh China's financial contribution and likely will for at least another decade. They also bring technical expertise and access to international organizations that China does not. Western states, the United States in particular, have an ability to assist African states in their security challenges in ways that China lacks. Despite the troubled colonial past, African states have deep political, security, and cultural ties to Western states that will endure. Africa's need for investment is too large and growing market presence too significant to be monopolized by any single party; China will not supplant U.S. and other Western influence in Africa.

China's global soft-power efforts have had decidedly mixed or disappointing results. For example, China's soft-power offensive in Southeast Asia was greatly feared ten years ago, but mismanagement and conflict with other Chinese interests moderated the success of Beijing's regional soft-power initiatives.[31] China's African relations bring many challenges that may prove difficult to reconcile; Africa brings language barriers and cultural differences, as well as nascent populist movements already pushing against Chinese actors. While Beijing's influence will be stronger with governments and business interests, its relationship with African civil society and African communities is likely to continue to be comparatively weak. Ties that are so dependent

[31] C. Richard Neu, "U.S. 'Soft Power' Abroad Is Losing Its Punch," Commentary, *U.S. News & World Report*, February 8, 2013.

on economic linkages and elite communities may prove more shallow and fickle than expected, particularly as China's growing investment begins to moderate. These also limit China's ability to influence political events, as evidenced by China's awkward silence in response to the Arab Spring.[32]

China will neither leave Africa nor become a dominant force there. Rather, China will remain as a major player with some dissimilar interests to the traditional major foreign powers, and the continent is unlikely to return to the higher levels of solely Western influence seen between the end of the Cold War and the rise of engagement by China and the other BRIC states. African states are likely to be selective consumers—embracing Chinese finance, infrastructure, and traditions of nonaccountability while seeking U.S. finance, security contributions, and political partnership. Even if African economic development continues apace, the results for Africa's political development will continue to be difficult to predict. Should U.S. critics be proven correct that China's approach of economic partnering without political and civil society considerations portends instability or public anger, China's approach may prove self-defeating. Similarly, the most enduring limitation to the problematic aspects of Chinese influence in Africa would be the success of the Washington Consensus and the demonstrated growth and stability of America's African partnerships.

Reinvigorate U.S. Diplomatic and Economic Engagement with Africa

To support U.S. leadership and buoy international norms, the United States should focus on reinvigorating its African relationships rather than competing with China in Africa. China's level of bilateral outreach with African states need not be matched, but the United States could initiate deeper ties with African states at senior and middle levels. While the Chinese FOCAC brings Beijing in regular contact with African heads of state, the United States hosted its first summit for African heads of state in August 2014. While U.S. Department of Defense engagement with African states has been comparatively robust, larger and more-

---

32 Kenneth M. Pollack, *The Arab Awakening: America and the Transformation of the Middle East,* Washington, D.C.: Brookings Institution, 2011, pp. 298–304.

senior efforts from the Departments of Agriculture, Energy, and Treasury would be welcome additions. In economic diplomacy, opening (or reopening) U.S. Foreign Commercial Service offices in Africa may help match some of China's expanded market share.

Distinguish Between PLA Crisis Reaction and Condition-Shaping Capabilities

The United States Africa Command (AFRICOM) should carefully evaluate PLA capability growth in Africa. Military leaders should assess growing PLA capabilities, in terms of likely missions. There is a critical distinction between forces designed and scaled to react to crises (NEOs, humanitarian assistance, disaster relief, limited site security, limited counterterrorism, and military partnering) and those attempting to shape security conditions. Should Beijing express interest in and create capabilities for implementing regime change, military deterrence, large-scale amphibious warfare, and significant long-range airlift, such capabilities would indicate a decidedly different security approach. Should the PLA seek reliable refueling locations, storage for naval provisions, and locations for limited military capabilities to react to crises, U.S. leaders should not consider these to be threatening to American interests.

Insulate Sino-American Relations in Africa from Broader Geopolitical Tensions

The United States should seek to insulate Sino-American relations in Africa from broader currents in the bilateral relationship that tend to be dominated by the far more intense security competition in the Asia-Pacific region. U.S. decisionmakers should strive to prevent disagreements over security interests in Africa from disturbing the broader Sino-American relationship. Conversely, to the extent possible, exogenous variables—such as rising tensions in China's maritime periphery, or over Korean or Iranian issues—should be isolated from U.S.-China interactions in Africa. Allowing outside events to color the Sino-American relationship within Africa risks a de facto and unnecessary horizontal escalation of tensions into a region largely characterized by civilian interactions. Such a dynamic would also reinforce the perception or reality of great-power rivalry. The United States requests that China depoliticize military-to-military relations that have frequently been interrupted when Beijing takes offense to U.S. actions, such as arms sales to Taiwan. In a similar way, AFRICOM should insulate its interactions with China from disagreements between the states elsewhere.

Seek Opportunities for Cooperation with China in Africa

AFRICOM should seek opportunities for greater engagement with the PLA in Africa. The emerging security threats that the PLA will face in Africa are familiar to the Joint Force, particularly the Army, opening the potential for meaningful exchanges between the respective services. Despite deep levels of strategic distrust (particularly from Beijing), the PLA is likely to face challenges that it is unprepared to answer. Much as the United States organizes cooperation with Western and host-nation militaries over noncombatant evacuation, humanitarian assistance, and disaster relief operations, inviting participation or observation from the PLA may have benefits. Such a move undercuts containment rhetoric, demonstrates the value of lessened tensions, and lessens anxiety in African capitals over great-power rivalry. How to structure, target, and calibrate such an effort is a matter for further research; such research would ideally join a deep understanding of the PLA's interservice dynamic, strategic culture, and debate on emerging security challenges with more operational-level research in the key regions where China's security needs are likely to become acute.

The U.S. Army is best-positioned among the services to lead such an engagement initiative. While the relationship of both countries' navies and air forces are focused on the more conflicting dimensions of anti-access/area denial and AirSea Battle in the Pacific theater, the two ground forces have more shared interests and fewer direct areas of conflict. The PLA Army is historically the preeminent service within the Chinese military establishment, but the focus on the Pacific theater has increased the focus on China's maritime periphery and on its navy, air force, and missile assets (organized outside the PLA Army under the Second Artillery Corps). Africa may be the most promising theater in which to pursue diplomacy with China through military-to-military relationships. The U.S. Army can bring much to this role, given its long history of attaché and military diplomacy contributions. An explicit, consistent policy of inviting greater collaboration with China in Africa may be AFRICOM's strongest contribution to the Joint Force's Pacific challenges.

References

African Center for Economic Transformation, *Looking East: China-Africa Engagements—Ghana Country Case Study*, Accra, Ghana, December 2009. As of December 8, 2014:
http://acetforafrica.org/wp-content/uploads/2010/08/Looking-East-Ghana-China-Case-Study-2010.pdf

Agence France-Presse, "Anthropologist Jane Goodall: China Is Pillaging Africa Like an Old Colonial Power," Raw Story, February 17, 2014. As of January 15, 2015:
http://www.rawstory.com/rs/2014/02/anthropologist-jane-goodall-china-is-pillaging-africa-like-an-old-colonial-power/

Akkermans, Joost, "China Plans 45 Billion Yuan Media Expansion, Morning Post Says," *Bloomberg*, January 12, 2009.

Al Jazeera, "Kidnapped Chinese Workers Freed in Sudan," *Al Jazeera English*, February 7, 2012. As of January 1, 2014:
http://www.aljazeera.com/news/africa/2012/02/20122718057383606.html

Allen, Kenneth W., and Eric A. McVadon, *China's Foreign Military Relations*, Washington, D.C.: Henry L. Stimson Center, 1999.

Alves, Ana, "China's Economic Statecraft," *Journal of Current Chinese Affairs*, Vol. 42, No. 1, 2013, pp. 99–130.

Amnesty International, *People's Republic of China: Sustaining Conflict and Human Rights Abuses: The Flow of Arms Accelerates*, New York: Amnesty International, 2006.

AsiaNews, "Weapons for Ivory: The Illegal Trade Between Bejiing and Zimbabwe," November 17, 2004. As of December 8, 2014:
http://www.asianews.it/news-en/Weapons-for-ivory:-the-illegal-trade-between-Bejiing-and-Zimbabwe-1918.html

Associated Press in Beijing, "Chinese State Media Slam Hillary Clinton's Speech in Africa," *The Guardian*, August 3, 2012. As of June 26, 2014:
http://www.theguardian.com/world/2012/aug/03/hillary-clinton-china-africa-investment

Atkinson, Joel, "Gambia's Break with Taiwan," *The Diplomat*, December 2, 2013. As of December 8, 2014:
http://thediplomat.com/2013/12/gambias-break-with-taiwan/

Balfour, Frederik, "A Global Shopping Spree for the Chinese—Mainland Companies Are Snapping Up More Overseas Assets," *BusinessWeek*, November 18, 2002.

Bandurski, David, "How China Reports the Arab World," *China Media Project: University of Hong Kong*, April 18, 2011.

Baynton-Glen, Sarah, *Beyond Trade—China-Africa Investment Trends*, Standard Chartered Bank, Global Research, GR12JA, February 22, 2012.

BBC, "African Union Opens Chinese-Funded HQ in Ethiopia," January 28, 2012a. As of December 8, 2014:
http://www.bbc.com/news/world-africa-16770932

———, "Zambian Miners Kill Chinese Manager During Pay Protest," August 5, 2012b. As of January 1, 2014:
http://www.bbc.co.uk/news/world-africa-19135435

———, "BBC World Service to Lose 73 Jobs," October 18, 2012c. As of February 12, 2014:
http://www.bbc.com/news/entertainment-arts-19988316

———, "Gambia Severs Diplomatic Ties with Taiwan," November 15, 2013a. As of December 29, 2013:
http://www.bbc.com/news/world-africa-24951115

———, "South Sudan Crisis: East Africa Would Not Accept Coup," December 27, 2013b. As of December 8, 2014:
http://www.bbc.com/news/world-africa-25523946

Bloomberg News, "China's Wen Blocked by Politics From Fixing 'Unstable' Economy," March 3, 2010. As of February 3, 2014:
http://www.bloomberg.com/apps/news?pid=newsarchive&sid=aXZH3kF06hsY

———, "China's Africa Role Under New Scrutiny as Miners Expelled," June 7, 2013. As of January 1, 2014:
http://www.bloomberg.com/news/2013-06-06/chinese-county-warns-locals-from-going-to-ghana-to-mine-for-gold.html

BP, *BP Statistical Review of World Energy*, June 2012. As of December 8, 2014:
http://www.bp.com/content/dam/bp/pdf/Statistical-Review-2012/statistical_review_of_world_energy_2012.pdf

Brautigam, Deborah, "Chinese Workers Data: Anecdotes & Data," *China in Africa: The Real Story,* blog post, undated. As of June 27, 2014: http://www.chinaafricarealstory.com/p/chinese-workers-in-africa-anecdotes.html

———, *The Dragon's Gift: The Real Story of China in Africa,* Oxford: Oxford University Press, 2009.

———, "Africa's Eastern Promise," *Foreign Affairs,* January 2010a.

———, "African Traders in China and Substandard Goods," *China in Africa: The Real Story,* blog post, October 21, 2010b. As of June 27, 2014: http://www.chinaafricarealstory.com/2010/10/african-traders-in-china-and.html

———, "Chinese Development Aid in Africa: What, Where, Why, and How Much?" in Ligang Song and Jane Golley, eds., *Rising China: Global Challenges and Opportunities,* Canberra, Australia: Australian National University, 2011.

———, "China's Foreign Aid: The Economist Still Doesn't Get It," *China in Africa: The Real Story,* blog post, January 22, 2012. As of December 8, 2014: http://www.chinaafricarealstory.com/2012/01/chinas-foreign-aid-economist-still.html

———, "China in Africa: Really Rubbery Numbers," *China in Africa: The Real Story,* blog post, March 30, 2013a. As of June 27, 2014: http://www.chinaafricarealstory.com/2013/03/china-in-africa-really-rubbery-numbers.html

———, "Chinese Investment in Africa: How Much?" *China in Africa: The Real Story,* blog post, September 28, 2013b. As of December 30, 2013: http://www.chinaafricarealstory.com/2013/09/chinese-investment-in-africa-how-much.html

———, "Chinese Aid: How Much?" *China in Africa: The Real Story,* blog post, October 13, 2013c. As of December 8, 2014: http://www.chinaafricarealstory.com/2013/10/chinese-aid-how-much.html

Brautigam, Deborah, and Tang Xiaoyang, "African Shenzhen: China's Special Economic Zones in Africa," *Journal of Modern African Studies,* Vol. 49, No. 1, 2011, pp. 27–54.

Broadman, Harry G., and Isik Gozde, *Africa's Silk Road: China and India's New Economic Frontier,* Washington, D.C.: World Bank, 2007.

Brown, David E., *Hidden Dragon, Crouching Lion: How China's Advance in Africa Is Underestimated and Africa's Potential Underappreciated,* Carlisle, Pa.: Strategic Studies Institute, U.S. Army War College, 2012.

Cheru, Fantu, and C. I. Obi, eds., *The Rise of China and India in Africa: Challenges, Opportunities and Critical Interventions,* London: Zed, 2010.

Chileshe, Chilufya, *Chinese Debt, Aid and Trade: Opportunity or Threat for Zambia?* Occasional Paper, South African Institute of International Affairs, December 2010.

China Internet Information Center, "China Mapping Out the 11th Five-Year Development Guidelines," website, China.org, undated. As of January 15, 2015: http://www.china.org.cn/english/features/guideline/156529.htm

Chinese Central Television, "Chinese President Hu Delivers Keynote Speech at China-Africa Meeting," July 19, 2012. As of December 8, 2014: http://english.cntv.cn/program/newsupdate/20120719/108207.shtml

Chirwa-Ngoma, Joan, "Sata Praises Chinese," *The Post* (Zambia), April 7, 2013.

CNN Wire, "China Denies Report, Says It Did Not Sell Weapons to Libya," September 6, 2011. As of December 8, 2014: http://www.cnn.com/2011/WORLD/africa/09/05/libya.war/

Collins, Gabe, and Andrew Erickson, "The PLA Air Force's First Overseas Operational Deployment," *China Signpost*, March 1, 2011.

Cooper, Cortez A., *The PLA Navy's "New Historic Missions," Expanding Capabilities for a Re-Emergent Maritime Power*, Santa Monica, Calif.: RAND Corporation, CT-332, 2009. As of December 8, 2014: http://www.rand.org/pubs/testimonies/CT332.html

Craft, Cassidy, and Joseph P. Smaldone, "The Arms Trade and the Incidence of Political Violence in Sub-Saharan Africa, 1967–97," *Journal of Peace Research*, Vol. 39, No. 6, 2002, pp. 693–710.

DefenceWeb, "Chinese Peacekeepers Arrive in Mali in Historic Deployment," December 11, 2013. As of December 8, 2014: http://www.defenceweb.co.za/index.php?option=com_content&view=article&id=33029:chinese-peacekeepers-arrive-in-mali-in-historic-deployment&catid=56:diplomacy-a-peace&Itemid=111

Deitz, Ton, Kjell Havnevik, Mayke Kaag, and Terje Oestigaard, eds., *African Engagements: Africa Negotiating an Emerging Multipolar World*, Boston, Mass.: Brill Publishers, 2011.

Downs, Erica, "The Chinese Energy Security Debate," *The China Quarterly*, Vol. 177, March 2004, pp. 21–41.

———, "The Fact and Fiction of Sino-African Energy Relations," *China Security*, Vol. 3, No. 3, 2007, pp. 42–68.

———, "China's 'New' Energy Administration," *China Business Review*, November 2008, pp. 42–45.

———, "Who's Afraid of China's Oil Companies?" in Carlos Pascual and Jonathan Elkind, eds., *Energy Security: Economics, Politics, Strategy, and Implications*, Washington, D.C..: Brookings Institution, 2009, pp. 73–102.

The Economist, "Africa and China: More Than Minerals," March 23, 2013.

Eisenman, Joshua, Eric Heginbotham, and Derek Mitchell, *China and the Developing World: Beijing's Strategy for the Twenty-First Century*, Armonk, N.Y.: M.E. Sharpe, 2007.

Engineering News-Record, "The Top 250 International Contractors," web page, 2013. As of June 27, 2014:
http://enr.construction.com/toplists/Top-International-Contractors/001-100.asp

Erickson, Andrew, "China's Political and Security Challenges in the Middle East," testimony before the U.S.-China Economic and Security Review Commission hearing on China and the Middle East, June 6, 2013.

Erickson, Andrew, and Gabe Collins, "China's Oil Security Pipe Dream," *Naval War College Review*, Vol. 63, No. 2, 2010, pp. 89–111.

Erickson, Andrew, and Austin Strange, *No Substitute for Experience: Chinese Antipiracy Operations in the Gulf of Aden*, Newport, R.I.: China Maritime Studies Institute, U.S. Naval War College, No. 10, October 2013a.

———, "China and the International Antipiracy Effort," *The Diplomat*, November 1, 2013b. As of January 1, 2014:
http://thediplomat.com/2013/11/
china-and-the-international-antipiracy-effort/?allpages=yes

———, "Piracy's Next Frontier: A Role for China in Gulf of Guinea Security?" *The National Interest,* December 10, 2013c. As of December 8, 2014:
http://nationalinterest.org/commentary/
piracy's-next-frontier-role-china-gulf-guinea-security-9533

———, "China and the Far Seas," *The Diplomat*, January 10, 2014.

Ernst & Young Global Limited, *Natural Gas in Africa: The Frontiers of the Golden Age*, 2012. As of December 8, 2014:
http://www.ey.com/GL/en/Industries/Oil---Gas/
Natural-gas-in-Africa-frontier-of-the-Golden-Age

Fallon, Amy, "Throwing the Tanzania-Zambia Railway a Lifeline," *Inter Press Service*, December 11, 2013. As of September 8, 2014:
http://www.ipsnews.net/2013/12/tanzania-zambia-railway-line-time-stands-still

Finkelstein, David Michael, Michael A. McDevitt, and Mark A. Ryan, eds., *Chinese Warfighting: The PLA Experience Since 1949*, Armonk, N.Y.: M.E. Sharpe, Inc., 2003.

Fleeson, Lucinda, "Bureau of Missing Bureaus," *American Journalism Review*, October/November 2003.

Ford, Peter, "Why Chinese Workers Are Getting Kidnapped Abroad," *The Christian Science Monitor*, February 1, 2012. As of January 1, 2014: http://www.csmonitor.com/World/Asia-Pacific/2012/0201/Why-Chinese-workers-are-getting-kidnapped-abroad

Fortin, Jacey, "China in the Middle: South Sudan's Biggest Oil Importer Learns to Wield Its Clout," *International Business Times*, April 9, 2014.

Gadzala, Aleksandra, and Marek Hanusch, *African Perspectives on China-Africa: Gauging Popular Perceptions and Their Economic and Political Determinants*, Afrobarometer Working Paper No. 117, January 2010.

Gamache, Lauren, Alexander Hammer, Lin Jones, "China's Trade and Investment Relationship with Africa," U.S. International Trade Commission, Executive Briefings on Trade, April 2013.

GAO—*See* U.S. Government Accountability Office.

Ghost, Palash, "Zambia Seizes Chinese-Owned Mine Over Poor Safety Record: The Fraying Relations Between Beijing And Africa," *International Business Times*, February 21, 2013.

Grimmett, Richard F., "Conventional Arms Transfers to Developing Nations, 2002–2009," Washington, D.C.: Congressional Research Service, CRS Report for Congress, September 10, 2010.

The Guardian, "Chinese State Media Slam Hillary Clinton's Speech in Africa," August 3, 2012. As of September 18, 2013: http://www.theguardian.com/world/2012/aug/03/hillary-clinton-china-africa-investment

Haizhou, Zhang, "Protection of Overseas Chinese Citizens and Assets Proposed," *China Daily,* March 9, 2012.

Haroz, David, "China in Africa: Symbiosis or Exploitation," *Fletcher Forum of World Affairs*, Vol. 35, No. 2, 2011, pp. 65–88. As of December 8, 2014: http://www.fletcherforum.org/wp-content/uploads/2013/12/Haroz_FA.pdf

Hartnett, Daniel, "China's First Deployment of Combat Forces to a UN Peacekeeping Mission–South Sudan," Washington, D.C.: U.S.-China Economic and Security Review Commission, Staff Memo, March 13, 2012.

Heaton, Paul, "Oil for What?—Illicit Iraqi Oil Contracts and the U.N. Security Council," *Journal of Economic Perspectives*, Vol. 19, No. 4, 2005, pp. 193–206.

Helmut, Reisen, *Is China Actually Helping Improve Debt Sustainability in Africa?* Policy Brief, Intergovernmental Group of Twenty-Four on International Monetary Affairs and Development, 2008.

Herberg, Mikkal, "China's Maritime Disputes in the East and South China Seas," testimony before the U.S.-China Economic Security Review Commission, Washington, D.C., January 26, 2012.

The Heritage Foundation and American Enterprise Institute, "China Global Investment Tracker," Washington, D.C., 2012. As of December 8, 2014: http://www.heritage.org/research/projects/china-global-investment-tracker-interactive-map

Huang, Yasheng, "China's Great Rebalancing: Promise and Peril," McKinsey and Company, June 2013.

Human Rights Watch, *Stoking the Fires: Military Assistance and Arms Trafficking in Burundi*, New York: Human Rights Watch Arms Project, December 1997.

IMF—*See* International Monetary Fund.

Institute for Security Studies and the African Forum and Network on Debt and Development, *ISS Workshop Report: National Consultation on Mapping Chinese Development Assistance in Africa: An Analysis of the Experiences of Ethiopia*, Addis Ababa, Ethiopia, July 30, 2012.

International Monetary Fund, "Direction of Trade Statistics (DOTS)," web tool, undated. As of December 8, 2014: http://elibrary-data.imf.org/FindDataReports.aspx?d=33061&e=170921

Information Office of the State Council, *China's Peaceful Development Road*, White Paper, Beijing: Ministry of National Defense of the People's Republic of China, December 22, 2005. As of December 8, 2014: http://www.china.org.cn/english/2005/Dec/152669.htm

———, *China's National Defense in 2006*, White Paper, Beijing: Ministry of National Defense of the People's Republic of China, 2006. As of January 15, 2015: http://eng.mod.gov.cn/Database/WhitePapers/2006.htm

———, *China-Africa Economic and Trade Cooperation 2010*, White Paper, Beijing, December 23, 2010a. As of January 15, 2015: http://www.china.org.cn/government/whitepaper/node_7107834.htm

———, *China's National Defense in 2010*, White Paper, Beijing: Ministry of National Defense of the People's Republic of China, 2010b. As of January 15, 2015: http://eng.mod.gov.cn/Database/WhitePapers/2010.htm

———, *China's Foreign Aid*, White Paper, Beijing, April 2011.

———, *The Diversified Employment of China's Armed Forces*, White Paper, Beijing: Ministry of National Defense of the People's Republic of China, April 2013a. As of January 15, 2015: http://eng.mod.gov.cn/Database/WhitePapers/2012.htm

———, *China-Africa Economic and Trade Cooperation 2013*, White Paper, Beijing, August 2013b. As of January 15, 2015: http://www.china.org.cn/government/whitepaper/node_7189938.htm

International Energy Agency, *World Energy Outlook 2012*, Paris, November 12, 2012.

IOSC—*See* Information Office of the State Council.

Jacobs, Andrew, "Pursuing Soft Power, China Puts Stamp on Africa's News," *New York Times*, August 16, 2012.

Jaegar, Markus, *Sino-U.S. Relations: Economic Deterrence and Asymmetric Vulnerability*, Deutsche Bank Research, 2010.

The Jamestown Foundation, *China Brief*, Vol. 11, No. 15, August 12, 2011. As of January 15, 2015:
http://www.jamestown.org/uploads/media/cb_11_33.pdf

———, *China Brief*, Vol. 12, No. 10, May 11, 2012. As of January 15, 2015:
http://www.jamestown.org/uploads/media/cb_05_02.pdf

Jeuck, Lukas, *Arms Transfers to Zimbabwe: Implications for an Arms Treaty*, Stockholm International Peace Research Institute, Background Paper, March 2011. As of December 8, 2010:
http://books.sipri.org/files/misc/SIPRIBP1103.pdf

Jiang, Julie, and Jonathan Sinton, *Overseas Investments by Chinese National Oil Companies: Assessing the Drivers and Impacts*, International Energy Agency, Information Paper, February 2011.

Jopson, Barney, "BRICs in Africa: Adding It up," *Financial Times*, Beyond BRICs blog, August 5, 2010. As of December 8, 2014:
http://blogs.ft.com/beyond-brics/2010/08/05/76851/

Kandu, Frank, "China to Build New Malawi Stadium," *BBC Sport*, October 31, 2012. As of December 8, 2014:
http://www.bbc.com/sport/0/football/20153471

Kansteiner, Walter H., III, and J. Stephen Morrison, *Rising U.S. Stakes in Africa: Seven Proposals to Strengthen U.S.-Africa Policy*, Washington, D.C.: Center for Strategic and International Studies, Report of the Africa Policy Advisory Panel, May 2004.

Kapchanga, Mark, "Changing Channels: The Rise of Chinese Media in Africa," *Think Africa Press*, February 17, 2013. As of February 12, 2014:
http://www.thinkafricapress.com/society/
changing-channels-rise-chinese-media-africa

Kimenyi, Mwangi Kimenyi, and Zenia Lewis, "The BRICs and the New Scramble for Africa," in *Foresight Africa: The Continent's Greatest Challenges and Opportunities for 2011*, Washington, D.C.: Brookings Institution, Africa Growth Initiative, 2011, pp. 19–21.

Kleine-Ahlbrandt, Stephanie, and Andrew Small, "China's New Dictatorship Diplomacy: Is Beijing Parting with Pariahs?" *Foreign Affairs,* Vol. 87, No. 1, 2008, pp. 38–56.

Kong, Bo, *China's International Petroleum Policy*, Santa Barbara, Calif.: Praeger Security International, 2009.

Kostecka, Daniel, "Places and Bases: The Chinese Navy's Emerging Support Network in the Indian Ocean," *Naval War College Review,* Vol. 64, No. 1, Winter 2011, pp. 59–78. As of January 28, 2015:
http://www.usnwc.edu/getattachment/0ecf6fde-e49e-485a-b135-c240a22e8a13/Places-and-Bases--The-Chinese-Navy-s-Emerging-Supp

Leveret, Flynt, and Jeffrey Bader, "Managing China U.S. Energy Competition in the Middle East," *The Washington Quarterly*, Vol. 29, No. 1, 2005, pp. 187–201.

Lewis, Steven, "China's Maritime Disputes in the East and South China Seas," testimony before the U.S.-China Economic Security Review Commission, Washington, D.C., April 4, 2013.

Lieberthal, Kenneth, and David M. Lampton, *Bureaucracy, Politics, and Decision Making in Post-Mao China*, Berkeley, Calif.: University of California Press, 1992.

Lieberthal, Kenneth, and Jisi Wang, *Addressing U.S.-China Strategic Distrust*, Washington, D.C.: Brookings Institution, John L. Thornton China Center, 2012.

Lin, Li-Wen, and Curtis Milhaupt, "We Are the (National) Champions: Understanding the Mechanisms of State Capitalism in China," *Stanford Law Review,* Vol. 65, 2013, pp. 697–761.

Loro, Horta, "Defense and Military Education: A Dimension of Chinese Power," *Power and Interest News Report*, September 29, 2006.

Lyons, Roy, "The USSR, China and the Horn of Africa," *Review of African Political Economy,* Vol. 5, No. 12, 1978, pp. 5–30.

Manson, Katrina, "China Hits Back at Clinton's Africa Comments," *The Washington Post*, August 3, 2012. As of June 26, 2014:
http://articles.washingtonpost.com/2012-08-03/world/35491940_1_china-hits-south-sudan-xinhua-news-agency

McCarthy, Terry, "China's Aggressive Stance Reveals Lack of Coordination," *Yale Global*, December 5, 2012. As of January 1, 2014:
http://yaleglobal.yale.edu/content/chinas-aggressive-stance-reveals-lack-coordination

McKenzie, David, "Chinese Media Making Inroads into Africa," CNN, September 25, 2012.

Medecins Sans Frontieres, *Violence, Health, and Access to Aid in Unity State/Western Upper Nile, Sudan*, Holland, April 2002, p. 16. As of October 30, 2014:
http://www.msf.fr/sites/www.msf.fr/files/2002-04-01-MSFH.pdf

Medeiros, Evan S., *Analyzing China's Defense Industries and the Implications for Chinese Military Modernization*, Santa Monica, Calif.: RAND Corporation, CT-217, 2004. As of December 8, 2014:
http://www.rand.org/pubs/testimonies/CT217.html

———, *China's International Behavior: Activism, Opportunism, and Diversification*, Santa Monica, Calif.: RAND Corporation, MG-850-AF, 2009. As of December 8, 2014:
http://www.rand.org/pubs/monographs/MG850.html

Menzie, W. David, "China's Quest for Resources," testimony before the U.S.-China Economic and Security Review Commission hearing on "China's Global Quest for Resources and Implications for the United States," January 26, 2012. As of September 18, 2013:
http://www.doi.gov/ocl/hearings/112/ChinaMinerals_012612.cfm

Mertha, Andrew, "Fragmented Authoritarianism 2.0: Political Pluralization in the Chinese Poly Process," *The China Quarterly*, Vol. 220, 2009, pp. 995–1012.

Mian, Yang, and Song Fei, "Further Reminding the Chinese Enterprises and Workforces in Africa of the Risks and Necessary Safety Measures," *Asia and Africa Review*, Vol. 2, 2012.

Miles, Donna, "U.S., Chinese Navies Exercise Counterpiracy in Gulf of Aden," American Forces Press Service, August 26, 2013.

Ministry of Commerce of the People's Republic of China, "Foreign Investment," website, various years. As of January 15, 2015:
http://english.mofcom.gov.cn/article/statistic/foreigninvestment/

Ministry of Foreign Affairs of the People's Republic of China, "Forum on China-Africa Cooperation," web page, undated. As of February 3, 2014:
http://www.focac.org/eng/

———, "Vice Premier Wang Yang Meets with Zimbabwean Prime Minister Morgan Tsvangirai," Beijing, May 23, 2013. As of February 3, 2014:
http://www.mfa.gov.cn/eng/wjdt/wshd/t1044750.shtml

Ming, Xia, "'China Threat' or a 'Peaceful Rise of China'?" *The New York Times*, undated.

Muekalia, Domingos Jardo, "Africa and China's Strategic Partnership," *African Security Review*, Vol. 13, No. 1, 2004, pp. 5–11.

Mulvenon, James C., *Soldiers of Fortune: The Rise and Fall of the Chinese Military-Business Complex, 1978–1998*, Armonk, N.Y.: M. E. Sharpe, 2001.

———, "Chairman Hu and the PLA's 'New Historic Missions,'" *China Leadership Monitor*, 2009.

Murray, Craig, *China to Deploy "Security Force" to UN Peacekeeping Operation in Mali*, Washington, D.C.: U.S.-China Economic and Security Review Commission, Staff Research Backgrounder, July 9, 2013. As of December 8, 2014: http://www.uscc.gov/sites/default/files/Research/Backgrounder_China%20to%20Deply%20Security%20Force%20to%20UN%20Peacekeeping%20Operation%20in%20Mali_0.pdf

Musakwa, Tendai, "Deborah Brautigam Discusses the US and China's Relations with Africa," The China Africa Project, April 8, 2013. As of June 27, 2014: http://www.chinaafricaproject.com/deborah-Brautigam-discusses-the-us-and-chinas-relations-with-africa/

Nathan, Andrew J., and Andrew Scobell, *China's Search for Security*, New York: Columbia University Press, 2012.

Neu, C. Richard, "U.S. 'Soft Power' Abroad Is Losing Its Punch," Commentary, *U.S. News & World Report*, February 8, 2013. As of December 8, 2014: http://www.rand.org/blog/2013/02/us-soft-power-abroad-is-losing-its-punch.html

Ng'wanakilala, Fumbuka, and George Obulutsa, "China's Xi Tells Africa He Seeks Relationship of Equals," *Reuters*, March 25, 2013.

Nossiter, Adam, "U.S. Engages with an Iron Leader in Equatorial Guinea," *New York Times*, May 30, 2011.

Obayuwana, Oghogho, "China Wants to Partner Nigeria on Gulf of Guinea," *The Guardian* (Nigeria), August 2, 2012.

Office of the Secretary of Defense, *Annual Report To Congress: Military and Security Developments Involving the People's Republic of China 2014*, U.S. Department of Defense, April 24, 2014. As of December 8, 2014: http://www.defense.gov/pubs/2014_DoD_China_Report.pdf

Ojakorotu, Victor, and Ayo Whetho, "Sino-African Relations: The Cold War Years and After," *Asia Journal of Global Studies*, Vol. 2, No. 2, 2008, pp. 35–43.

Organisation for Economic Co-Operation and Development, "OECD Statistics," web tool, undated. As of January 15, 2015: http://stats.oecd.org

Oxford Analytica, "New Challenges Arise as China-Africa Ties Deepen," January 2013. As of January 14, 2014: https://www.oxan.com/display.aspx?ItemID=DB180925

Pan, Wei, *Zhongguo Mo Shi: Jie Du Renmin Gongheguo De 60 Nian* [*China Model: A New Developmental Model from the Sixty Years of the People's Republic*], Beijing: Zhong Yang Bian Yi Chu Ban She, 2009.

Payne, Richard J., and Cassandra R. Veney, "China's Post-Cold War African Policy," *Asian Survey*, Vol. 38, No. 9, 1998, pp. 867–879.

People's Daily Online, ed., "Overseas Chinese Firms Face Security Risks," February 6, 2012a. As of December 8, 2014:
http://en.people.cn/90883/7720977.html

———, "China Will Run Short of 25 Kinds of Minerals by 2020," February 27, 2012b. As of December 8, 2014:
http://en.people.cn/90778/7739687.html

People's Republic of China, *China's African Policy*, Beijing, January 12, 2006. As of January 15, 2015:
http://www.gov.cn/misc/2006-01/12/content_156490.htm

———, *Twelfth Five-Year Plan*, trans. Delegation of the European Union in China, March 2011. As of January 15, 2015:
http://www.britishchamber.cn/sites/default/files/full-translation-5-yr-plan-2011-2015.doc

Petroleum Intelligence Weekly, "Eager Chinese Pay Dearly for Foreign Assets," April 29, 2002.

Pew Global Attitudes Project, "Global Unease with Major World Powers: 47-Nation Pew Global Attitudes Survey," Pew Research Center, Public Opinion Survey, June 27, 2007.

Pham, Peter, "Assessing China's Role and Influence in Africa," testimony before the Committee of Foreign Affairs hearing for the Subcommittee on Africa, Global Health, and Human Rights, March 29, 2012. As of September 18, 2013:
http://www.gpo.gov/fdsys/pkg/CHRG-112hhrg73538/html/CHRG-112hhrg73538.htm.

Pollack, Kenneth M., *The Arab Awakening: America and the Transformation of the Middle East*, Washington, D.C.: Brookings Institution, 2011.

Puska, Susan, "Military Backs China's African Adventure," *Asia Times*, June 8, 2007.

Rahman, Maseeh, "Chinese Plans in Seychelles Revive Indian Fears of Encirclement," *The Guardian*, March 23, 2012. As of January 1, 2014:
http://www.theguardian.com/world/2012/mar/22/china-seychelles-indian-fears-encirclement

Ratner, Ely, "The Emergent Security Threats Reshaping China's Rise," *The Washington Quarterly*, Vol. 34, No. 1, 2011, pp. 29–44.

Reed, Douglas, *The Battle for Rhodesia*, Cape Town, South Africa: Haum, 1966.

Refugees International, *Sudan: Oil Exploration Fueling Displacement in the South*, Bulletin, June 14, 2006. As of December 8, 2014:
http://www.refworld.org/docid/47a6eeda1d.html

Reuters, "Clinton Warns Against 'New Colonialism' in Africa," June 11, 2011. As of June 26, 2014:
http://www.reuters.com/article/2011/06/11/us-clinton-africa-idUSTRE75A0RI20110611

Rong, Jin, "Nation Told to Bolster Domestic Consumption," *China Daily*, November 4, 2006. As of February 3, 2014:
http://www.chinadaily.com.cn/china/2006-11/04/content_724473.htm

Rotberg, Robert I., ed., *China into Africa: Trade, Aid, and Influence*, Washington, D.C.: Brookings Institution, 2008.

Roxburgh, Charles, Norbert Dörr, Acha Leke, Amine Tazi-Riffi, Arend van Wamelen, Susan Lund, Mutsa Chironga, Tarik Alatovik, Charles Atkins, Nadia Terfous, and Till Zeino-Mahmalat, *Lions on the Move: The Progress and Potential of African Economies*, McKinsey Global Institute, June 2010.

Sautman, Barry, and Yan Hairong, "African Perspectives on China-Africa Links," *China Quarterly*, Vol. 199, September 2009, pp. 728–759.

Scobell, Andrew, and Andrew J. Nathan, "China's Overstretched Military," *The Washington Quarterly*, Fall 2012.
http://csis.org/files/publication/twq12FallScobellNathan.pdf

Shalmon, Dan, and Henry Lee, "Searching for Oil: China's Oil Strategies in Africa," in Robert Rotberg, ed., *China into Africa: Trade, Aid, and Influence*, Washington, D.C.: Brookings Institution, 2008.

Shek, Colin, "Chinese Media Expands Africa Presence," Al Jazeera, January 24, 2013. As of February 12, 2014:
http://www.aljazeera.com/indepth/features/2013/01/201312071929822435.html

Shinn, David H., "Military and Security Relations: China, Africa, and the Rest of the World," in Robert I. Rotberg, ed., *China into Africa: Trade, Aid, and Influence*, Washington, D.C.: Brookings Institution, 2008.

———, "The Impact of China's Growing Influence in Africa," *The European Financial Review*, April 2011a, pp. 16–19.

———, "China's Growing Role in Africa: Implications for U.S. Policy," testimony before the Senate Committee on Foreign Relations Subcommittee on African Affairs, November 1, 2011b.

———, "China-Africa Relations: The Big Picture," *International Policy Digest*, December 6, 2011c. As of December 8, 2014:
http://www.internationalpolicydigest.org/2011/12/06/china-africa-relations-the-big-picture/

———, "China's Investments in Africa," China-U.S. Focus, November 1, 2012. As of December 8, 2014:
http://www.chinausfocus.com/finance-economy/chinas-investments-in-africa/

———, "China and Africa in the Xi Jinping Era," *The Diplomat*, March 25, 2013.

Shinn, David H., and Kerry Brown, *Africa Programme Meeting Summary—China and Africa: A Century of Engagement*, London: Chatham House, June 29, 2012.

Shinn, David H., and Joshua Eisenman, *China and Africa: A Century of Engagement*, Philadelphia, Pa.: University of Pennsylvania, 2012.

Shirk, Susan L., *China: Fragile Superpower*, Oxford: Oxford University Press, 2007.

Singh, Mandip, "China Base a Threat to India Navy?" *The Diplomat*, December 17, 2011.

Starr, John Bryan, *Understanding China: A Guide to China's Economy, History, and Political Structure*, New York: Hill and Wang, 2001.

Stockholm International Peace Research Institute, "Arms Transfers Database," web tool, undated. As of December 8, 2014:
http://www.sipri.org/databases/armstransfers

Talbot, Brent J., "The Transatlantic Gap over Iraq," *European Security*, Vol. 17, No. 1, 2008, pp. 61–84.

Taylor, Ian, *The International Relations of Sub-Saharan Africa*, New York: Continuum, 2010.

———, "China's Arms Transfers to Africa and Political Violence," *Terrorism and Political Violence*, Vol. 25, 2013.

Torode, Greg, "PLA Delays Taking Lead on Piracy," *South China Morning Post*, June 21, 2010. As of January 1, 2014:
http://www.scmp.com/article/717692/pla-delays-taking-lead-piracy

UNCTAD—*See* United Nations Conference on Trade and Development.

United Nations, "Comtrade Database," web tool, undated(a). As of December 8, 2014:
http://comtrade.un.org

———, "Financing Peacekeeping. United Nations Peacekeeping," web page, undated(b). As of September 8, 2014:
http://www.un.org/en/peacekeeping/operations/financing.shtml

———, *Disarmament Yearbook 2006*, Vol. 31, New York: Office for Disarmament Affairs, 2007.

United Nations Conference on Trade and Development, "Statistics," web tool, undated(a). As of December 8, 2014:
http://unctad.org/en/Pages/Statistics.aspx

———, "UNCTADstat," web tool, undated(b). As of January 15, 2015:
http://unctadstat.unctad.org/EN/

United Nations Peacekeeping, "Troop and Police Contributors," web tool, undated. As of January 15, 2015:
http://www.un.org/en/peacekeeping/resources/statistics/contributors.shtml

U.S. Department of State, "A Guide to the United States' History of Recognition, Diplomatic, and Consular Relations, by Country, Since 1776: Equatorial Guinea," Office of the Historian, undated. As of December 8, 2014:
https://history.state.gov/countries/equatorial-guinea

———, "U.S. Relations with Equatorial Guinea: Fact Sheet," Bureau of African Affairs, April 1, 2013.

U.S. Energy Information Administration, *China Country Analysis Brief*, Washington, D.C.: U.S. Department of Energy, April 22, 2013a.

———, "Overview Data for China," web page, May 30, 2013b. As of December 8, 2014:
http://www.eia.gov/countries/country-data.cfm?fips=CH

———, "Overview Data for United States," web page, May 30, 2013c. As of December 8, 2014:
http://www.eia.gov/countries/country-data.cfm?fips=us

———, *Country Analysis Brief: Sudan and South Sudan*, Washington, D.C.: U.S. Department of Energy, September 5, 2013d.

U.S. Geological Survey, *2012 Minerals Yearbook: China*, Washington, D.C.: U.S. Department of the Interior, December 2013. As of December 8, 2014:
http://minerals.usgs.gov/minerals/pubs/country/2012/myb3-2012-ch.pdf

———, *2012 Minerals Yearbook: Africa*, Washington, D.C.: U.S. Department of the Interior, December 2014. As of December 8, 2014:
http://minerals.usgs.gov/minerals/pubs/country/2012/myb3-sum-2012-africa.pdf

U.S. Government Accountability Office, *Sub-Saharan Africa: Trends in U.S. and Chinese Economic Engagement*, Washington, D.C., GAO-13-199, February 2013.

USGS—*See* U.S. Geological Survey.

U.S. Office of Naval Intelligence, *Horn of Africa and Gulf of Guinea: Piracy Analysis and Warning Weekly (PAWW) Report*, Maritime OPINTEL Report, December 19, 2013. As of January 15, 2015:
http://www.oni.navy.mil/Intelligence_Community/piracy/pdf/20131218_PAWW.pdf

Vandiver, Frank E., *Shadows of Vietnam: Lyndon Johnson's Wars*, College Station, Tex.: Texas A&M University Press, 1997.

Victor, David, "What Resource Wars?" *The National Interest,* December 2007.

Vogel, Ezra F., *Deng Xiaoping and the Transformation of China*, Cambridge, Mass.: Harvard University Press, Belknap Press, 2011.

Voice of America, "U.S. to Open 'Mini Embassy' in Equatorial Guinea," November 19, 2002. As of December 8, 2014:
http://www.voanews.com/content/a-13-a-2002-11-19-14-us-67410252/383403.html

Wa, Zhou, "Warships to Help Dispose of Syrian Chemical Weapons," *China Daily USA*, December 26, 2013. As of February 12, 2014:
http://usa.chinadaily.com.cn/epaper/2013-12/26/content_17198885.htm

Walter, Carl E., and Fraser J. T. Howie, *Red Capitalism: The Fragile Financial Foundation of China's Extraordinary Rise*, Singapore: Wiley, 2011.

Wei, Xu, "More Consideration Given to Guards for Overseas Workers," *China Daily*, February 22, 2012. As of December 8, 2014:
http://www.chinadaily.com.cn/china/2012-02/22/content_14662657.htm

Weisbrod, Aaron, and John Whalley, "The Contribution of Chinese FDI to Africa's Pre Crisis Growth Surge," National Bureau of Economic Research Working Paper 17544, October 2011.

Weitz, Richard, "China and Africa Peacekeeping," Second Line of Defense, March 2013. As of January 15, 2015:
http://www.sldinfo.com/china-and-african-peacekeeping/

Wenzhi, Gao, "Work by Mutual Efforts to Promote Trade And Economic Collaboration Between Ghana and China," remarks to Standard Chartered Bank professional forum, Accra, Ghana, October 1, 2013.

When China Met Africa, dir. Marc Francis and Nick Francis, Speakit Films, October 2011.

Wines, Michael, and Betsy Apple, "Beijing Says Qaddafi Officials Sought Chinese Arms Supplies," *New York Times*, September 5, 2011. As of December 8, 2014:
http://www.nytimes.com/2011/09/06/world/asia/06china.html?_r=0

Wing, Terry, "Clinton Answers China's Challenge in Africa," Voice of America, August 1, 2012. As of June 26, 2014:
http://www.voanews.com/content/clinton-answers-chinas-challenge-in-africa/1452812.html

Wudu, Waakhe Simon, "UN Speeds up Deployment as Fighting Rages in S. Sudan" *The Daily Star* (Lebanon), December 27, 2013. As of January 3, 2014:
http://www.dailystar.com.lb/News/International/2013/Dec-27/242399-un-speeds-up-deployment-as-fighting-rages-in-ssudan.ashx

Xiaokun, Li, "Navy Looks at Offer from Seychelles," *China Daily*, December 13, 2013. As of January 1, 2014:
http://www.chinadaily.com.cn/china/2011-12/13/content_14254395.htm

Xinhua, "Chinese Envoy Briefs UN on China-Africa Relations," September 11, 2007. As of December 8, 2014:
http://www.un.org/africa/osaa/press/China-Africa%20Relations.pdf

———, "CPC Sets Targets for 12th Five-Year Program," Information Office of the State Council and the China International Publishing Group, October 27, 2010. As of February 3, 2014:
http://www.china.org.cn/china/2010-10/27/content_21214648.htm

———, "International Disaster Relief Operations Obligation of China's Armed Forces," China.org, March 31, 2011. As of January 15, 2015:
http://www.china.org.cn/china/2011-03/31/content_22265927.htm

———, "China's Development Model Good Example for African Nations: CCM Vice-Chairman of Tanzania," June 21, 2012a. As of December 8, 2014:
http://news.xinhuanet.com/english/china/2012-06/20/c_131665186.htm

———, "China to Announce New Measures on Cooperation with Africa: Vice FM," *China Radio International English*, July 12, 2012b. As of December 8, 2014:
http://english.cri.cn/6909/2012/07/12/3241s711565.htm

———, "U.S. Plot to Sow Discord Between China, Africa Is Doomed to Fail," August 3, 2012c. As of December 8, 2014:
http://news.xinhuanet.com/english/indepth/2012-08/03/c_131759593.htm

———, "Two Killed in Northern Nigeria," *China Daily*, October 8, 2012d. As of January 1, 2014:
http://www.chinadaily.com.cn/world/2012-10/08/content_15801435.htm

———, "Chinese Killed by Boko Haram Suspects in Nigeria," *China Daily*, October 9, 2012e. As of December 8, 2014:
http://usa.chinadaily.com.cn/world/2012-10/09/content_15802238.htm

———, "One Chinese Worker Shot Dead in Northern Nigeria," *China Daily*, October 20, 2012f. As of January 1, 2014:
http://www.chinadaily.com.cn/china/2012-10/20/content_15833253.htm

———, "At Least 4 Killed, Several Injured in Northern Nigeria Church Explosion," *NZweek*, October 28, 2012g. As of January 1, 2014:
http://www.nzweek.com/world/
at-least-4-killed-several-injured-in-northern-nigeria-church-explosion-18509/

———, "135 Chinese Peacekeepers Arrive in Capital of Mali," *CRIEnglish*, December 5, 2013a.

———, "UN Slams Deadly Attack on Peacekeepers in Mali," December 15, 2013b. As of January 6, 2014:
http://news.xinhuanet.com/english/world/2013-12/15/c_132968350.htm

Yergin, Daniel, "Ensuring Energy Security," *Foreign Affairs*, Vol. 85, No. 2, March/April 2006, pp. 69–82.

Yihan, Hu, "China Has No Colonial Designs on Africa," *China Daily*, December 9, 2011.

Yueh, Linda, "China's 'Going Out, Bringing In' Policy: the Geo-Economics of China's Rise," International Institute of Strategic Studies Geo-Economics and Strategy Seminar, *A New Era of Geo-Economics: Assessing the Interplay of Economic and Political Risk*, March 25, 2012.

Zhang, Lili, "An Analysis of China's All-Out Efforts to Evacuate Chinese Nationals from Libya," *Contemporary World*, April 5, 2011.

Zhimin, Chen, and Jian Junbo, *Chinese Provinces as Foreign Policy Actors*, Braamfontein, South Africa: South African Institute of International Affairs, Occasional Paper No. 22, January 2012.